Released Outward

Released Outward

Liberating Congregations To Do Justice, Love Mercy, and Live Faithfully

by
David Lowry

WIPF & STOCK · Eugene, Oregon

RELEASED OUTWARD
Liberating Congregations To Do Justice, Love Mercy, and Live Faithfully

Wipf & Stock
An Imprint of Wipf and Stock Publishers
199 W. 8th Ave., Suite 3
Eugene, OR 97401

www.wipfandstock.com

PAPERBACK ISBN: 978-1-5326-4072-8
HARDCOVER ISBN: 978-1-5326-4073-5
EBOOK ISBN: 978-1-5326-4074-2

Manufactured in the U.S.A.

Contents

Preface

I HAVE SERVED TWO congregations as pastor. The first was a largely work-ing-class Lutheran congregation, of primarily Swedish ancestry, located in a white enclave on Chicago's south side. I served this congregation for about four-and-a-half years. The second, also Lutheran, was an African-American congregation on Chicago's south side. I served this congregation for almost twenty-nine years. Common to both was the issue of how to respond to God's reign and operate in the ways of God's governance.

Each had idols to turn from, in order, as Paul says, "to serve the true and living God." Among the first congregation's idols was that of racism; among the second's, classism. In order to be a people outwardly directed in mission to all people, we needed to repent and be released from that which had us enslaved. We were like addicts who needed to get to the third step in the twelve-step program: the step of surrender made available by the grace of God.

The backdrop of this book is primarily my almost-three-decades of experience with St. Thomas, the second of the congregations mentioned above. We underwent a change that moved us from a one hour a week on Sunday inward orientation to an outward mission that oriented us to our neighborhood. This outward orientation included ministries to children, addicts (and their families), those who had been abused, and the home-less. We were (and St. Thomas continues to be) a small urban congrega-tion that had come to respond to God's call outward in programs such as a year-round children's program and homework center, recovery ministries, community gatherings (where every Wednesday through Friday evening in August we served food and brought our worship outside into our court-yard), New Beginnings Gatherings that gave a forum for seekers, various kinds of Bible studies open to all, and training for ministry. Our ministry included determined engagement on issues of social justice through a faith-based community organization.

The change we experienced was spiritual; it was a shifting of centers. It had to do with being delivered from false attachments. We were stuck on ourselves or various elements of ourselves. We needed to lose our lives for Christ's sake and for the sake of the gospel. We needed, in the language of the twelve-step program, to "turn our wills and our lives over to the care of God." When it came to being a community of Jesus' followers, our lives—in twelve-step language—had become unmanageable. We had to come to a place where we realized we were bound and helpless to liberate ourselves. We needed God's deliverance. We came to experience that deliverance and realize that every form of liberation is grounded in God's action and grace.

This book began as a presentation for the Annual Martin Luther King Jr. Day Celebration of the Albert "Pete" Pero Jr. Multicultural Center at the Lutheran School of Theology at Chicago. The subject of that talk was "The Local Church and the Common Good." The preparation, the lecture, and the lively sharing that followed brought focus to the question concerning the kind of change necessary for congregations to move outward. I realized I had more to say.

Acknowledgments

THIS BOOK COULD NOT have been written without the St. Thomas community of faith. In this body of Christ, in the African-American neighborhood of South Shore on Chicago's south side, I changed. I matured. My children were loved, nurtured, and grew up. It was the entirety of the experience at St. Thomas that has fed my writing—the joys and sorrows, the dying and rising, the new life, the struggle, and the overcoming. It was this community's love, a love poured out by the Holy Spirit. It is hard to name names and not leave others out, but when I name these names everyone in the St. Thomas community will understand: Deacon Sharon Briggs, Deacon Rochelle Wilson, and my wife, Elly. I give thanks to God for these leaders, among the many ministers that have carried on the mission of God's good news at St. Thomas.

When I first came to St. Thomas, there were a number of young African-American pastors who were called to various African-American Lutheran churches on Chicago's south side. They were a godsend for me, a white pastor serving one of these congregations. They generously and freely gave guidance and help. In those early years, I especially think of Robert Gant, Reginald Hansome, Raymond Legania, Stephen Marsh, Tyrone Partee, and Booker Vance. Pastor Vance, in particular, was a partner in ministry for most of the years I was at St. Thomas, and shared in the ministry of training lay leaders. We have had many long conversations about the church's mission in the world. Also, Lawrence Clark, Rayford Grady, and Cheryl Pero, along with Pastor Legania and myself, are involved in the Liberating Leadership Diaconal Training. These pastors and many others across denominations have had an influence on my ministry, and therefore on this work.

I am grateful for the readers of early manuscripts: Vickie Johnson, the current pastor of St. Thomas; William Hall, the pastor of St. James Lutheran

ACKNOWLEDGMENTS

Church, where I am a member; Frank Showers, who is a pastor and spiritual director; Byron Meline, who has pastored churches in rural Minnesota; and my daughter, Elizabeth Lowry, who is an associate pastor in a large suburban church in Ohio. Their comments and discussion improved this book. I am also very grateful for my sister-in-law, Lorilea Jaderborg, who did a preliminary and much-needed editing of my manuscript. Finally, I am grateful for the help I received with the last steps of this process from Matthew Wimer, Caleb Shupe, and the people of Wipf and Stock.

1

Introduction

IN ITS BEGINNINGS, THE church was a movement that the book of Acts describes as turning the world upside down. Local churches were gatherings for the sake of the outward movement of the gospel, which was seen as the power of God to rescue and liberate. The church in its beginnings, and at times of awakening and crisis, has brought change not only to individuals and families, but to societies and the world.

In contrast, for many of us in mainline historic churches, our experience of the church as it concretely exists today often feels less like a movement and more like a keeper of morals and traditions, many of which are very local and ethnic in nature, its outwardness consisting in sporadic "charity work." Rather than a movement bringing the gospel to a hurting world, we often see local churches operating as institutions where councils meet to work on how they are going to enhance *their* worship, *their* music ministry, *their* programs directed to the families of *their* church. Rather than praying and shaping strategies for its mission, many church councils meet primarily to contrive ways to keep the lights on and pay the bills so that the programs and traditions of the church can continue. Ask these questions: Where is the church and where are local congregations in the outward movement of good news proclamation and action such that they confront, agitate (think of Jesus overturning tables), heal and deliver? Where and how are local assemblies of God effecting liberating change in the lives of individuals, families, neighborhoods and society? Where and how are they letting justice roll down like waters, being merciful in practical, meaningful ways? Where and how are they moving out beyond local traditions and internal church programs?

Ask a further question: *How* do insulated and isolated congregations come out of themselves and become part of a movement that brings healing to individuals and families, deliverance to those bound, and effects change directed toward a just society? Without diminishing the importance of faith for the individual and family good, and its significance for the wider society, how do we become a people actively and concretely working for the larger common good, seeing beyond our families and neighborhoods and congregations? Or, more to the point, how do we come to see ourselves, our families and congregations in light of the transforming power of God so that we are useful channels of healing and liberation to individuals *and* the community, to personal relationships *and* the common good. They are, after all, of one piece.

In other words, how do congregations change? How do they move from an inward orientation to an outward mission? How do they become ambassadors proclaiming the message of reconciliation to God and neighbor? How do they come to love mercy and do justice and walk humbly where God leads them? How do they come to care about the good of all? How do congregations become salt, light, and yeast, sharing not only the gospel but themselves in serving others and effecting movements for justice and change?

How do they move beyond defensive postures and reactionary impulses to become servants, who look beyond faults and see needs—who, with Jesus, are not in the world to condemn but be used as God's instruments to seek and to save the lost? How do churches move beyond their own contexts to see the other and the needs of the other? How are their contexts enlarged so that they no longer see the other through the lens of preconceptions and prejudices but actually begin to see themselves *in* the other? How can such solidarity be made possible so that they truly enter into the lives of others and the life of this world—no longer viewing from the outside, but deeply engaged?

At a gathering of urban pastors involved in faith-based community organizing, an African-American pastor in the United Methodist Church asked how we can involve urban and suburban churches in the movement to radically change the criminal justice system. We were meeting to work on ways to respond to the massive injustice of the American criminal justice system, as seen in the mass incarceration of people of color and the poor. The pastor asking about suburban and rural church involvement was reflecting on his experience at conference gatherings where a broad spectrum of congregations often brought to the forefront the disunity felt in the distance between Christians. Therefore, the question: How can there be a truly diverse movement? The underlying expectation is that the church, because of its common vision, ought to be involved, with all its diversity, in a common mission. The United States of America needs to hear one word, from the one church, of many peoples. As Dietrich Bonhoeffer said in a sermon to an ecumenical conference in 1934, the world needs to hear "a whole word, not a half word." Nor does it need to hear a different word from suburban, rural and urban churches. A word needs to go out from the church that calls all to the liberating movement towards a just community.[1]

The vision of a diverse but united movement is a great attraction; we experience a taste of it here and there, but to a large extent the reality escapes us. Considering the question raised by the African-American urban pastor mentioned above, we raise an additional and necessary question: How does the privileged Christianity of white America move from its comfort with a privileged position in order to recognize the urgent need to do for the sake of all the work of making right what is wrong? How can those, whose privileged status has meant that they do not have to acknowledge such status, come to address their actual poverty and have their eyes opened, to recognize what it is that truly restores what is broken?

Clearly what is needed is transformation—change at a radical level. Any notion of God's acceptance without transformational, liberating change sounds like a theology for middle-class, comfortable Christians who are content with an hour on Sunday, if it does not disturb their lives and ideologies. But for people experiencing oppression, the gospel of liberating power is critical for life.

Of course, the liberating gospel is critical for all people who are bound by idolatries and addictions that make them incapable of seeing the needs of others, moving outward as agents of change, bearing good news to the poor and caring about a truly just society. People who are active in their addictions (that which has them stuck) need to know that there is a road to recovery, that it is possible to change.

Old "mainline" denominations like my own have tended to be high on vision and low on response. We study, exegete, analyze, and interpret; we even examine our hermeneutical methodology, which is to say we spend

1. Bonhoeffer, *Testament To Freedom*, 229.

time examining what we are doing when we are interpreting. But if we are strong on attending to the vision, we are weak on the side of the call for response.

We tend to have a general understanding of the vision: Jesus proclaimed the reign of God and was the bearer of that reign, and we receive into our lives both message and bearer and become participants in that reality. When we proclaim God's reign, we join Jesus in proclaiming God's way of governing, that which exalts those who are humbled and humbles those who are exalted; which makes the last, first and the first, last; which makes the servant, the leader. Jesus, who is servant of all, instructs his followers not to lord it over one another, but rather humbly wash each other's feet. We are to love one another as Jesus has loved us—and this is directly connected to loving God "with all our heart, soul, strength, and mind."

This beautiful reality of God's reign of love moves outward to all. It is global. It is about the common good. It is about the sharing of our lives. It is about serving. We get indications of it wherever we see justice, mercy, and faith manifested.

One of the issues that leaders in congregations face, however, is the issue of moving from the general grand message to the lived lives of those who gather to hear the message. The message has to get increasingly concrete, speaking to the contexts of people's lives—not only the ones they choose to recognize for themselves, but the wider context of the society and world in which they live.

We have to lift up what Jesus, following Micah, calls the weightier matters of the law, doing justice, loving mercy, and walking by faith.[2] These marks of our true humanity, which as Christians we are to exhibit, can act as a mirror for the congregations we serve. What does "being the church" look like where we serve? Is it turned inward, focused on that which will maintain its own fellowship and traditions—the equivalent to the Pharisees' preoccupation with tithing mint, dill, and cummin? Is the church we serve doing justice and loving mercy that is outward-directed? What form does "doing justice and loving mercy" look like, more concretely, in the context of the wider society? Can we get specific?

What I am imagining is a change in our local congregations, such that living under God's governance manifests itself in concrete, specific ways that affect what is actually happening in the lives of others and our society,

---

2. Matt 23:23. Unless otherwise noted, the New Revised Standard Version (NRSV) is used in this book when citing Scripture.

so that justice and mercy are actually being done. We must not simply be talking grand talk, but actually making right what is wrong so that real lives are truly being affected and people from many places and experiences are sharing in the work.

For that to happen, we need the whole church in all its expressions. Many of us, after all, have given great care to the vision, but we have had blind spots when it comes to the content and the concrete actions necessary to truly affect the situations of others and our society. We need the help of others. Dietrich Bonhoeffer discovered the need for this at Abyssinian Baptist Church in Harlem. Reggie Williams, in his book *Bonhoeffer's Black Jesus: Harlem Renaissance Theology and an Ethic of Resistance*, outlines the transformation of Bonhoeffer's theology by the Black Jesus he encountered at Abyssinian in 1930–1931. Bonhoeffer experienced a different kind of centrality of Christ from that of the colonialist Eurocentric form of Christianity. He said, in fact, that he received very little from Union Theological Seminary. It was at Abyssinian in Harlem that his theology was radicalized. It was only there, in his first four months, that he said he heard a genuine proclamation of the gospel. And he said he was "increasingly discovering greater religious power and originality among" African-Americans.[3] He was discovering Christ and the Reign of God modeled among the oppressed—in spirit and in truth. And it strengthened him for his own witness and martyrdom in Nazi Germany.

The vision we cast and the message we proclaim must become increasingly concrete in its call to do justice, love mercy, and walk humbly with our God. This can only happen as we listen to and join with the oppressed—those who are experiencing injustice—and encourage the members of our congregations to do the same. In doing this, we will be doing something counter-cultural and subversive—and bound to get us in trouble.

But casting the vision and proclaiming the message is only part of what must happen.

Jesus proclaimed the reign of God, described it, told stories about how God's reign operates and how one comes to experience God's reign. But Jesus also called for response: "Repent and believe for God's reign is at hand." The call for response is a call to change our minds, to move our trust from idols to serve a true and living God, to allow God to free us from our addictions and obsessions in order to do God's will. It is, of course, by God's grace that we turn around; nevertheless God has us participating.

3. Williams, *Bonhoeffer's Black Jesus*, Chapter 2, Section 5.

More than twenty-five years ago, I took about a dozen members of St. Thomas, an African-American congregation that I served, on the south side of Chicago, to a workshop on faith-based community organizing. It was a day-long event, and I had hopes for the involvement of my congregation in faith-based organizing. However, it was clear after the event that there was little interest. The attitude we had toward community organizing at that time was of one accord with the way we tended to think about evangelism. Evangelism was seen as recruiting members for the sake of our survival as a congregation, rather than as the outward movement of the gospel as the power to rescue people. Community organizing threatened to take us too much out of our inturned obsessions.

The reality was that we had every reason to care about the issues facing our community; they affected us. But we were in many ways stuck. For some, a little affluence had made it possible to isolate ourselves (at least to some extent) from the problems facing us. For others, the issue was survival, and the pressures, stress, and anxiety over managing daily tasks like simply getting food on the table. Such stress overwhelmed the ability to address the wider issues that were actually the underlying cause of a survivalist environment.

In the end, we had to name and address our idols. One of those, for us, was classism. We had to turn from being, as one of our neighbors described us when I first became pastor, an "elitist" church; we had to become a church for all people. We had to undergo a spiritual transformation before people in our neighborhood could see our church as truly community-oriented, open and welcoming to all.

The point is, we had to get unstuck and unattached. We had to do what Paul writes that the church in Thessalonica did: We had to turn "to God from idols, to serve a living and true God."[4] And we had to *keep* doing that.

At St. Thomas, an African-American congregation, we had to address classism. At a church for which I was previously pastor, in a white enclave on Chicago's south side, we had to address racism. I had to speak to it in sermons and conversations and engage us with the wider, diverse church. The neighborhood was on the verge of a change and the congregation was oblivious to it. The only way it would remain a congregation would be by repenting from racism. We needed to go to God to release us and to give us hearts that would welcome others with the welcome of Christ. There were a few who responded in a way that could be seen in the change taking place

---

4. 1 Thess 1:9.

in their lives, but on the whole, we resisted; and the neighborhood changed, some years after I left, as Mexican-Americans moved in. Another pastor helped the congregation to pass on their building and property to a new church venture oriented to the changing community. Eventually another church, made up of people of Mexican descent, bought the building. But the possibility was always there for the previous church, by God's grace and power, to change and to love in a way that transcends cultures, shares in our common human struggles, and welcomes diversity. We would have had to get unstuck, however, from considering *our* ways, *our* culture, *our* ideologies as the norm.

That which keeps us from the work of God's reign in relation to others in our broken and hurting world are our idolatries, addictions, and obsessions. It is that which we are stuck on and attached to that keeps us from our true selves, our true callings, and the true God. It is from these false attachments that we must keep turning—as the Shaker song has it: "Till by turning, turning we come 'round right."

Idolatry is much like addiction. As we became involved in a ministry to addicts and their families at St. Thomas, we came to realize that drug addiction was not the only addiction to which we were prey. Spiritually speaking, idolatry and addiction were very similar, and the twelve steps of the twelve-step program were for all of us, whether our addictions involved drugs or not. We all had to:

1. Admit that we were powerless over our addiction and that our lives had become unmanageable.

2. Come to believe that a Power greater than ourselves could restore us to sanity.

3. Make a decision to turn our will and our lives over to the care of God, as we understood God.

If our churches are going to be movements doing justice, loving mercy, and walking faithfully, being yeast that affects the world, we are going to have to address our idolatries and addictions, admit to our powerlessness, believe in a power greater than our own, and turn our wills and lives over to the care of God. (We cannot assume that this is what is happening simply because people show up in a church building.)

So, for example, how can white suburban and rural churches join urban churches of color in a movement to affect real change in our society? This question takes churches beyond simply financial support or helping in soup kitchens or other kinds of "charity" work. It involves us in structural change—working for more just societal systems, so that we diminish the need for soup kitchens. It involves changes in our mindset and how we look at others and welcome others.

How is it possible to see the whole, to recognize we are one with others distant from ourselves to the point that we are unified in action? The first step is to address the addictions. Address our "isms"—individualism, sexism, classism, ethnocentrism, and so on. In these United States of America, the church must address racism! One of the symptoms of addiction, of course, is denial, and racism in this country hides. That is why the first step toward recovery is admitting our addiction.

And racism is a good example of addiction. Like all addictions, it is a false attachment—in this case to whiteness or white ways of thinking, to Eurocentric cosmologies and philosophies, as a standard measure, regarding other viewpoints as negligible in value. This false attachment can be very subtle and deceptive. Like all addictions, it involves mind tricks. The addicted mind plays with us. In this case, it makes us think we really do not need those other viewpoints and that our thinking in this regard has nothing to do with racism—and so we are able to carry on with our addiction without acknowledging our problem. We remain stuck and do not receive the viewpoint from others from whom we most need it. And we are able to tell ourselves it is not because of racism.

When it comes to pastoral leadership, it is not primarily a matter of arguing with people over their ideologies—those are part of the mind tricks. Ideologies come from hidden biases, fears, and attachments—from our idols or addictions, and we use those ideologies to protect our idols and addictions. Sometimes we talk about the need for consciousness-raising—and there *is* a need for consciousness-raising. But until we start turning from our idols or are freed from our addictions, we have little openness for changing our ideologies. We have to speak to the idols, name the addictions, expose our obsessions, and get past the defensiveness we feel. And we must do so in such a way that we recognize our powerlessness. Gerald May, a psychiatrist, writes in his book *Addiction and Grace* of addiction often bringing us to our knees where we discover grace. He then quotes Paul: "My grace is all you need; my power finds full strength in weakness."[5]

From a place of helplessness, we "make a decision to turn our will and our lives over to the care of God, as we understand God." The call for

5. May, *Addiction & Grace*, 20.

response is a call for a radical turning (in Paul's words) "to serve a living and true God."

I have called addiction a false attachment, because it keeps us from our true attachment to God. It keeps us from loving mercy, doing justice, and walking humbly. Karl Rahner writes of an infinite openness that makes all perception and knowledge possible.[6] When that openness is unhindered, and therefore a trusting openness to God, to "incomprehensible mystery," we have eyes to see and ears to hear; we are hearers of the word. It is our false attachments that close us up, narrow our view, lock us into false ways of viewing ourselves, the world, and others; for they blind us to the loving compassion and action of God.

So, for example, white members of our congregations can hardly be expected to join movements for social justice or think differently about others unless the addiction of racism is confessed and the turning begins— "turning, turning til we come 'round right." I am using racism as a significant example of an addiction or false attachment that keeps us from seeing or responding to the needs of others and the condition of our society. But any addiction will get in the way; these addictions can include comfort, convenience, technology, possessions, control, our own self-image, pleasing others—in short, anything.

So, we must proclaim God's reign, lift up the vision of God's governance and then call for response—for confession and repentance. Make clear what has us stuck, what keeps us from God's liberating will—to do justice and love mercy and walk faithfully. That means that pastors and leaders must identify their own addictions. Those of us who are white leaders in the church must address our own racism; we have to be on that journey in which we acknowledge the privileges racism gives us, acknowledge the ways we have assumed whiteness—traditional white ways of thinking—to be a measure of others thinking. People in our congregations will be much more able to hear us, if they know we are not judging them, but rather that we, too, acknowledge that we are caught up in the same addictions. It is only because of God's mercy that we are beginning to see our addictions and to be set free from them. We, who are leaders in the church, are under call, therefore, to cast the vision and call for response, both for the sake of the church as a movement of God and for the health and healing of those under our care. For freedom, Christ has set us free. And that is the power

---

6. Rahner uses the term "pre-apprehension" as that which is foundational to all human knowing; see Rahner, *Foundations*, 31–39.

of the gospel. The movement from false dependencies to God is at the same time the movement to our neighbor and to the world with the liberating gospel.

Our addictions and idolatries break down our discipline to, as Julian of Norwich puts it, "rest in divine love," from which love of neighbor and discerning God's will and empowering action flows.[7] By God's grace, we are being healed and freed from addictions, so we can respond and do the work that arises from God's compassionate reign. We can reach out with loving action to bring God's healing to a broken world.

The focus of this book is congregational change: the movement from an inward orientation to an outward mission, becoming salt, light, and yeast, bringing healing to individuals, welcoming the stranger, showing mercy, responding to needs, and doing justice. I am interested in the fundamental task for pastors and leaders who are addressing transformation in their congregations. The task is basic and unsurprising: It has to do with casting the vision and calling for response.

7. Sanna, *All Shall Be Well*, Chapter 10.

2

Roots

These things, which even angels long to examine, have now been proclaimed to you by those who brought you the good news. They did this in the power of the Holy Spirit, who was sent from heaven. (1 Pet 1:12, CEB)

Repent, for the kingdom of heaven has come near. (Matt 3:2)

FOR CHANGE TO COME, the good news of God's governance must be proclaimed, the vision cast, and a response be forthcoming. The change is always a turning to God and away from other centers we imagine for our lives. At the root of all change that moves us back to God is Word and Spirit. The Word is not always spoken, but often embodied, made manifest by its incarnation in presence and action. The word that brings radical change is a radical word—both proclaimed and embodied. It is a word that comes from the root: the radical center; the source of all that is real.

I think of the witness laid down in Scripture as being like a spring of fresh water bubbling out of the ground before it picks up debris as it streams down a mountain side. Yes, the early witnesses had their own contaminants. And yes, there are gains made with the further experience of God's people as faith gathers clarity, wisdom and praxis. But, given the human condition, we also tend to gather and "baptize" into "the faith," our prejudices, culture-driven outlooks, ethnocentric ways, and displaced desires and values. We move away from the source, forget who we are, get anxious, and start trying to save and secure ourselves; as a result, we lose our way. Instead of responding to the needs of others and reaching out to others with the gospel, losing their lives for the sake of Christ, church members—out of anxiety—seek to recruit members from a diminishing group of interested people in order to sustain their programs and institutions. Denominations expend effort in marketing their brand and, in their attempt to secure their institutions, often end up with programs far removed from the realities of the people their congregations serve—especially when it comes to the "losing our lives" that we all must undergo.

We have to keep going back to our roots, to our origins, and bring the people we serve with us. Pastors and leaders must allow the gathered "church people" to feel the distance between our practice and beliefs and the root witness and message. At the same time, those who are new to the faith must hear the radical call back to God and neighbor with freshness and encouragement. They must hear that God's governance is not far away. It is near. It is graciously given. It is God's pleasure to give it to us. Therefore, "do not be afraid."[1] Turn and receive; be changed and blessed.

Jesus, the Human One, came anointed by God "to bring good news to the poor." He proclaimed release and recovery to the needy and declared a new social order with God's governance—in which what is wrong is set right.[2] We saw the signs of God's restorative way of governing in Jesus' ministry of healing, and in his compassion for those who "were harassed and helpless, like sheep without a shepherd."[3]

Jesus exemplifies the shepherding of God as Ezekiel envisions it. Jesus is the shepherd who seeks and brings back the lost, binds up their wounds, and strengthens them.[4] This is also what the community of God's people are called to manifest. Therefore, we must see ourselves in the mirror of this radical call of God, a call to which we are unable to respond without the power of the Spirit (that is, without grace).

We must see ourselves from the root witness and engage ourselves with the particularity of Jesus—his teaching and praxis. We must let it speak to our own particularity—our lived experience in the context of our time. At the same time, we must find in Jesus, as the Christ, our liberation into the life of our true humanity as it comes from God. Our lives must be incorporated into the kind of reality Jesus lived—but *now*, in *our* time and place. That is, we must come to be as Paul writes, "in Christ"—not only

1. Luke 12:32.
2. Luke 4:18–19.
3. Matt 9:35–37.
4. Ezek 34:15–16.

understood as Messiah and Anointed One anticipated within the concrete history of Israel, but as logos of God made flesh, the one who "holds all things together," as what some have called the "cosmic Christ."[5] In Christ, we are reconciled to God and neighbor and to all creation. We must, therefore, see ourselves—as in a mirror—in the life and teaching of Jesus and be rooted in his life as the Christ, the image of God. We must attend to, clarify and make accessible to the *ecclesia*[6] the particularity of Jesus and the universality of Christ.

The Particularity of Jesus

Jesus makes clear from the beginning of his mission to the people of Israel that he is about the reign of God. He announces the nearness of God's reign and calls people to respond. It is not enough to simply hear of God's nearness and his governance. Decisions must be made. Jesus warns people not to be like those invited to a wedding feast who give excuses for not responding and "make light of" the invitation, while going on with the usual business of life as they have structured it.[7] If we do not decide to turn back to God and to God's governance, we will find ourselves in the "outer darkness, where there will be weeping and gnashing of teeth." Outside of God's presence and reign, there is only darkness.

Jesus got specific with people—he offered no generalities from which they could squirm away. To a rich ruler whose money was his god, Jesus said, "Sell all that you own and distribute the money to the poor, and you will have treasure in heaven; then come, follow me."[8] To a man who wanted Jesus to intervene for him with his brother over the distribution of their inheritance, Jesus said, "Take care! Be on your guard against all kinds of greed; for one's life does not consist in the abundance of possessions."[9] To religious leaders filled with their own self-made righteousness, he said, "Go and learn what this means, 'I desire mercy, not sacrifice.' For I have come to call not the righteous but sinners."[10]

5. Col 1:16–17.

6. This New Testament Greek word for "assembly" or "congregation" is generally translated "church," which today gives little sense of the original meaning.

7. Matt 22:1–10.

8. Luke 18:18–25.

9. Luke 12:15.

10. Matt 9:3.

To a sinner who knew she was a sinner (society let her know!), Jesus said, "I do not condemn you. Go your way, and from now on do not sin again."[11] To the men standing around the woman, filled with self-satisfaction, as judges ready to condemn her to death, Jesus said, "Let anyone among you who is without sin be the first to throw a stone at her."[12] To a chief collector of taxes for the occupying power of Rome, one who had gotten rich from the oppression of his own people, but who was ripe for change as he sought out Jesus, the words to him were: "Zacchaeus, hurry and come down; for I must stay at your house today." As the crowd murmured about Jesus going to eat with a sinner, Zacchaeus said to Jesus, "Look, half of my possessions, Lord, I will give to the poor; and if I have defrauded anyone of anything, I will pay back four times as much." He had made up his mind, made a turning of his life, and made a decision. Jesus declared, "Today salvation has come to this house, because he too is a son of Abraham. For the Son of Man came to seek out and to save the lost."[13]

In every one of these situations, and many more, the reign of God was brought to bear upon particular lives in particular situations—and in each case a response was solicited. Jesus, proclaimer and bearer of God's reign, engaged individuals and groups in the concreteness of their lives and at the point where they had to decide, as Karl Barth puts it, "to accept or to reject the sovereignty of God."[14] They had to decide about God's reign in their own lives at the point where it mattered, where their commitments were made.

As with Jesus, so with the followers of Jesus and with the community of his followers. There is no add-on faith here, no acceptance of a form of Christianity that works with prior commitments, leaving them intact. God's reign comes to change everything. In Jesus, we see real ministry to real human beings, because he engages them where they are centered: at the point of their "ultimate concern."[15] This is also where ministry must reside in the church today, in order for it to be the *ecclesia* of God in reality.

---

11. John 8:11. This later addition to the Gospel of John carries with it the spirit of Jesus' life and mission as we have come to experience it through his sayings, parables, and actions in the synoptic gospels and in the spirituality of the fourth gospel.

12. John 8:7.

13. For the story of this encounter between Zacchaeus and Jesus, see Luke 19:9–10.

14. Barth, *Word of God and Word of Man*, 41.

15. Tillich, *Dynamics of Faith*.

In the witness of the Gospels, we see the Palestinian Jesus operating in the context of the power structures of his time. We see him come with the power of God, bearing with him the government of God. He acknowledges the structures ("Give therefore to the emperor the things that are the emperor's, and to God the things that are God's"), but he operates from another place of authority, so that those in positions of power ask him, "By what authority are you doing these things, and who gave you this authority?"[16] The source of his authority is critical for him. His "father in heaven" gives him his call and his power. He is sent from God. And all who follow him must learn to see themselves as sent from God.

Because he knows who sent him and who he is and from whence comes his authority, he is free to respond to leaders who would intimidate him by telling him that king Herod is out to kill him. Jesus says, "Go and tell that fox for me, 'Listen, I am casting out demons and performing cures today and tomorrow, and on the third day I finish my work.'"[17] In other words, I cannot give my time or attention to your plots and conspiracies; I have a mission, a calling, and must see it through.

It is no different for the community of Jesus' followers. The community has a mission, and when it experiences its calling and responds, it does not have time to be sidetracked. It has work to do. When it gets diverted from its mission, it is because it has forgotten what kind of community it is and to whom it belongs. Because of this, we who are of this community must keep before ourselves the particularity of Jesus—precisely because it reminds us of the kind of life to which we are called. We are too ready to imagine a Jesus conformed to our already-set agendas.

In a world that made much of self-glory, honor, and power, and avoided shame, Jesus spent his time with the lowly and the shamed. We see, in Jesus, God's kind of governance, as he goes out to the poor, needy, and oppressed. He is about the work of uplift—of healing and restoration and deliverance. His discourses with the worldly rich and powerful are, for the most part, confrontations. Jesus is the "sign that will be opposed" by the ways of this world and its governments.[18] When he speaks to power, it is generally with words of judgment and for the sake of those who are oppressed. He says of the scribes and the Pharisees, "They tie up heavy burdens, hard to bear, and lay them on the shoulders of others; but they themselves are unwilling to

16. Matt 21:23.
17. Luke 13:32.
18. Luke 2:34.

lift a finger to move them."[19] But to those who are carrying heavy burdens he offers himself: "Come to me, all you that are weary and are carrying heavy burdens, and I will give you rest. Take my yoke upon you, and learn from me; for I am gentle and humble in heart, and you will find rest for your souls. For my yoke is easy, and my burden is light."[20]

Jesus calls together a community of followers who are to extend the invitation to the weary and heavily burdened: Come and get rest in this community. Have burdens lifted here. Learn from those who are learning from the one who is humble of heart. In the witness of the Gospels, Jesus expects his followers to do what he does. He teaches them and sends them out to do what they can only do by the anointing of the Spirit: heal the diseased and deliver those oppressed by the devil. Jesus calls together a community that can only function by virtue of its true identity as the body of Christ, by the power of God's Spirit.

In this community, there is blessing. Blessed are the poor in spirit, and those who mourn, and the lowly, and those who hunger and thirst for righteousness, and the merciful, and the pure in heart, and the peacemakers, and those who are persecuted for justice's sake. Jesus gathers the needy and welcomes those who mourn. They now receive their comfort from the Comforter. Jesus draws to himself people hungry for righteousness and justice. He leads all to their true selves, as they come to experience their true humanity in him and experience the purifying of their hearts from that which is false. He gathers all who have been enemies toward God to reconciliation with God and therefore also with one another, so that they become peacemakers who are willing to suffer persecution for justice's sake.[21]

People who come into such a blessed community as described above find that they have to make a decision. It is difficult to remain among people who are discovering their true selves in God and not respond. It is difficult to remain among people for whom it is clear their comfort comes from God and continue to seek your own comfort in an addiction. It is difficult to remain among a people who live by the mercy of God and continue yourself to hold judgment and nurse grudges against others. It is difficult to remain among people who are discovering purity of heart, which is to "will one thing," that one thing being God's will, while persisting in fashioning your own agenda in and of yourself without God. It is difficult to remain

19. Matt 23:4.
20. Matt 11:30.
21. Matt 5.

in a community of clearly needy, broken people, who know their neediness and know that it is a neediness for God, without choosing between running to God in your own helplessness or taking your neediness somewhere else.

People who come into a community where all are welcome and where grace reigns and the logos of God is embodied and being put into practice have to decide. As God was bringing transformation to the community of St. Thomas, it was becoming apparent that visitors who continued to come to our gatherings ended up having to make decisions about their lives; there came a point at which they would either stay or leave. I think of a woman who visited us for a period of time. She was drawn to the love she experienced in the fellowship, but at the same time she had to rub shoulders with all kinds of people, including many recovering addicts. When she shared with me her self-righteous condemnations and disdain of her alcoholic husband, I realized she was being faced with a decision. She would either forgive and embrace those who struggle with addictions and join the fellowship, or she would leave. She left. I believe she, like the rich young man who came to Jesus, left sadly. She was not yet ready for change and for the acknowledgment of her own brokenness.

The community that Jesus gathers is becoming a community governed by God, by God's reign. Jesus tells his community what to expect of God's governance. He tells them that his followers operate differently from the ways of governing and the systems of power that exist in the world around us. Jesus' words to his first followers continue to be true for all who would follow him today: "You know that the rulers of the Gentiles lord it over them, and their great ones are tyrants over them. It will not be so among you; but whoever wishes to be great among you must be your servant, and whoever wishes to be first among you must be your slave." Then the connection is made to himself: "just as the Son of Man came not to be served but to serve, and to give his life a ransom for many."[22]

This is a community that does not bother with plaques on walls honoring this or that person for their service or contributions, as a way to stimulate others to support the program. Its aim is not to appeal to the pride of place and status, but to honor the needy and broken with gracious welcome and the healing love of God. It is a community of servants, who expect no thanks in response to their actions. Rather, as Jesus declares, they simply say, "We have done only what we ought to have done!"[23] These are

22. Matt 20:26–28.
23. Luke 17:7–10.

servants who also know that when their "master" Jesus comes, he will do what he always does: "he will fasten his belt and have them sit down to eat, and he will come and serve them." (Jesus is Lord of all because he is servant of all.) Under the governance of God's Spirit, this Jesus kind of community is becoming a people for others—especially for those who are "harassed and helpless, like sheep without a shepherd."[24]

It is also becoming a community of the committed. Jesus' call is radical. Life under God's reign demands our whole selves; our most intimate relationships and all that we have must come under God's rule. Anything that takes the place of God's reign in our lives pushes us away from the source and foundation of our lives. Since Jesus will only lead us to a life centered in God, our refusal to let go of the whole of our lives to God cuts us off from following him.[25]

Along with this letting go of our lives is the carrying of the cross. We must bear our suffering (and dying), rather than running from it or looking for escape hatches. Jesus tells us that we will suffer for his sake and the gospel. We are not greater than the one we follow. Those who persecuted Jesus will persecute us. And those who were responsive to Jesus' word will be responsive to us as we declare the same word.[26] As Jesus' followers give active witness to the good news of God, they will experience various kinds of reactions.[27] If everyone speaks well of us, that is a sign of faithlessness, "for that is what their ancestors did to the false prophets."[28] We are therefore, to bear with suffering and trust ourselves to God, as Jesus did.

Further, Jesus' calling and sending places us in the midst of broken, hurting people. We are to enter into their experience, weeping with those who weep and rejoicing with those who rejoice. We are to fight the good fight of faith, with weapons of the Spirit, against the forces that bring down others—forces from within and without. We are sent out as ministers of God's healing and deliverance to situations of dysfunction and turmoil, violence and breakdown, disease and disorder, injustice and oppression. Our cross awaits us there and we must take it up. The community of Jesus' followers gains practice in concretely taking up its cross.

24. Matt 9:36.
25. Luke 14:26–27, 33.
26. John 15:20.
27. Matt 5:11.
28. Luke 6:26.

We see in Jesus the source of this kind of community, for we see the source of Jesus' life and calling. We see it in his seeking solitude early in the morning to pray.[29] His followers, seeing how important prayer was to Jesus and how intimate his relationship with God, asked him to teach them to pray. He instructed them to pray like him: *Abba*, "dear father." They were to approach God with the same intimacy. And they were to go forth with the same power that sent, guided, and enabled Jesus: At his baptism, the Holy Spirit came upon him.[30] Jesus let others know that the Spirit they saw active in him was available to all who were receptive: "If you then, who are evil, know how to give good gifts to your children, how much more will the heavenly Father give the Holy Spirit to those who ask him!"[31]

The same Spirit that empowered Jesus, empowered his *ecclesia*: "When they had prayed, the place in which they were gathered together was shaken; and they were all filled with the Holy Spirit and spoke the word of God with boldness."[32] Some have said that the church of the future will be a church of mystics, which is to say that it will live from its source, as did the church in its beginnings. As present and future generations find that much of what their ancestors found in church could be found elsewhere (relationships, support, wisdom, moral structure), increasingly those who identify with Jesus would be centered in the reality of life lived from its source: open, receptive, and empowered. They would be on a spiritual journey of dying and rising, rather than a moral rectifying of their lives.

Jesus' proclamation and praxis was completed in his suffering and dying. About one third of each of the Gospels is dedicated to the suffering and death of Jesus. It is clear that not only his life, but his death as well, had critical significance. He "died as a ransom for many." In other words, his death had something to do with our being bought out of slavery. It had to do with our liberation. "If the Son makes you free, you will be free indeed."[33] Dying forms the central action of Jesus' life—just as it does ours. The cross, dying, losing, letting go, is the doorway to resurrection to new life and to our true selves.

In Jesus, we see our true humanity and true community as it comes from God. In the particularity of Jesus, and of the first Jesus communities,

29. Mark 1:35, 6:46.
30. Luke 3:22.
31. Luke 11:13.
32. Acts 4:31.
33. John 8:36.

and wherever, in the history of the church, we have seen the bright renewal of this Jesus kind of community, we are given a mirror to place before what we call church today. Reflect on Francis of Assisi and the community that surrounded him in the thirteenth century. Think of William J. Seymour and the Azusa Street Revival at the beginning of the twentieth century which produced a community that broke the "color line," as blacks and whites, rich and poor gathered in response to the outpouring of the Spirit. We have clear signs of the kinds of community that bear the likeness of Christ.

We must not shy away from holding up the mirror, for it calls us back to our true selves and true community. Of course, we have to interpret the messages and actions, as expressed in forms fitting to the Palestinian situation of the first century, into our own time and place. But we must be careful not to throw out the radical elements of commitment and mission, to which Jesus calls us, on the premise that they belong to a different time. When we do rid ourselves of those radical elements, it is generally to maintain middle-class values or an already set agenda whose priorities do not flow from God's reign and will. ("Thy kingdom come, thy will be done!")

Saint Francis of Assisi demonstrated to us how the radical reality of Jesus in the first century continues to be available in every century, in ways we may want to dismiss. Francis has been called a second Christ because of his similar renouncing of possessions, his becoming poor with the poor, taking up his cross, and depending on God for every aspect of his life, which showed forth God's compassion and mercy in works of healing and expressions of Spirit-authority, wise counsel, and a joy-filled life.[34]

Certainly, each person and community of faith has to seek God for what is appropriate for their way to live out Jesus' radical call. But pastors and leaders in the church must hold up the mirror of Jesus' particularity and make present his call to follow, keeping in mind that they often are speaking to a middle-class Christianity, whose affluence and values isolate and shield it from its mission and call to minister. We are still called by Jesus to go out "into the streets and lanes of the town and bring in the poor, the crippled, the blind, and the lame."[35] Of course, in doing so, in obedience to the one we follow, our lifestyles and priorities change.

People ache for the real, for what truly matters, and, therefore, for Jesus' radical call to commitment. Some of those people are in the church, some outside. Some inside and outside will turn away, but others will respond as

34. For a depiction of St. Francis as a "second Christ" see Rohr, *Eager to Love*.
35. Luke 14:21.

if their lives depended upon it (for they do!). But here we acknowledge that Jesus' life, teaching, and ministry, as it exemplifies who we are called to be in our true humanity, would overwhelm us, if it were not that Jesus was and is the Christ.

The Universality of Christ

The Gospels witness to Jesus as Messiah, Christ, God's Anointed. The notion of an anointed one as ruler is present in the scriptural witness, along with anticipation that God's anointed would come to liberate (redeem) Israel—a desire with political connotations.[36] There is a history to the idea of "messiah" that includes notions of a ruler (a son of God), a liberator of Israel from captivity to foreign power (a captivity that was often connected to Israel's disobedience, and therefore a deliverance that came with mercy and forgiveness). This history further includes the anticipation that Israel would be established above all the nations and that the nations would come to Zion to worship the true God. Jesus steps into this history and his death and resurrection move it forward. In the confession of the first Christians, "Jesus is Lord," his reign, which comes in the midst of this world's rulers and ways of ruling, is subversive, for its authority and power are exercised in a radically different manner and from a radically different source. Jesus, as God's Anointed (the king who brings in God's kingdom), is revealing and making present God's action. God is "with us" in Jesus, Emmanuel. I am particularly interested in this broader meaning of "Christ" as we have it in the Pauline letters and Hebrews and the Johannine writings, and its implication for the life of Jesus' followers and communities. I think of references to Christ as "the image of God" (2 Cor 4:4), as "the image of the invisible God" (Col 1:15), and "the reflection of God's glory and the exact imprint of God's very being" (Heb 1:3). With these words, we are reminded of the view of humanity in Genesis: "God created humankind in his image," and we are meant to see in Jesus, as the Christ, our true humanity.[37]

Furthermore, in Christ, who is the image of God in the flesh, "all things in heaven and on earth were created" (Col 1:16–17)." Consider also Philippians 2:6–8, where Christ is depicted as not holding on to the "form of God," but emptying himself and taking on human form. We read these passages, and we see in the idea of Christ something very much like

36. Luke 1:68, 2:38, 3:22, 24:21; Ps 2:7.
37. Gen 1:27.

what we encounter in the Gospel of John's prologue, where all things come into being through God's self-expression, which then becomes flesh (John 1:1–3, 14). The logos of God, God's expression or image, is the one through whom all things come to be and the one in whom "all things hold together" (Col 1:17). This one (Christians have learned to say the "second person of the Trinity") fills out the meaning of "Christ." All things were created "for him," humanity created and fitted to receive God's Image, Logos, Self-expression, in order that God's image and expression might shine forth in us. Understood in this way, Jesus, as the Christ, is Jesus as the union of God and humanity. He is our older brother (the "firstborn"), through whom we (and all humanity) are united with God, and without whom we lose our humanity. Our true selves are "hidden with Christ in God (Col 3:3)." In other words, to be human is to be divine, or "divinized" as the Eastern church has emphasized. It is possible to see in this "universality of Christ" the availability of this Christ reality to all humankind. It is an existential aspect of being human that includes the dynamic of dying and rising, by which we are transformed into our true selves, available to be received by grace as the gift of our humanity as it comes from God and is found in God.

All this is ours explicitly, as Paul tells us, "in Christ." We become like Christ ("little Christs") through Christ Jesus, God's logos joined to the flesh of our humanity, our humanity raised up into God. Through participation in Jesus as the Christ, we come to be our true selves as God created us to be. In Christ, we are raised with Christ "above all rule and authority and power and dominion, and above every name that is named, not only in this age but also in the age to come."[38] The radical call, the commitment of faith, the unconditional love, the hope in God, our union with God—all is ours in Christ, along with forgiveness, mercy, and necessary change. Therefore, we do not need to be overwhelmed by the radicalness of Jesus' call or fear the intimidation of the world, for, as Dietrich Bonhoeffer wrote from a Nazi prison, "everything depends on the words 'in Him.'"[39] The knowledge of this reality that is ours, in Christ, encourages us in the "midst of things we cannot understand" while facing evil that "threatens to undo us."[40]

38. Eph 1:21.

39. Bonhoeffer, *Letters and Papers*, Letter 192.

40. The first phrase comes from a funeral prayer in *Evangelical Lutheran Worship*. The second phrase comes from Luther's hymn, *A Mighty Fortress is Our God*.

In Christ there is reconciliation with God.[41] Our liberation from that which has kept us from God is a gift in Christ.[42] Being baptized into Christ Jesus, we participate in his death and resurrection so that we die to sin and are made alive to God.[43] God, of course, is the source of this life in Christ Jesus, and Christ in whom we live is our wisdom, righteousness, sanctification and redemption.[44] Faith itself comes to be ours in Christ Jesus as we share in his faith. ("We ourselves believed in Christ Jesus so that we could be made righteous by the faithfulness of Christ and not by the works of the Law.")[45]

This reality of participation in Christ must not be glossed over, if we desire to see the transformation of the church today into a people for others. We are released outward through Christ, whose movement is outward in self-emptying and entering into our suffering and weakness. Being *in* this Christ reality changes us. This is a contrast to what we experience in many churches today. Here, communal life and mission are built largely on the foundation of, on the one hand, giving assent to "being saved by grace through faith" and, on the other hand, doing those things we recognize as "good" within the limits of our inturned visions and biases. Our assent to God's salvation is disconnected from our Christian practice. The connection between "being saved" and living the Christ-life is lost.

If our vision is going to be enlarged, we must go deeper, undergo transformation, be changed from "one degree of glory to another."[46] I have heard recovering addicts, as they move through the twelve steps, encourage one another with the words, "more will be revealed." And more *is* revealed, as they continue taking steps in this spiritual program. Christians understand this when they view themselves in Christ and know they must participate more deeply in this Christ reality. Of course, going deeper into Christ means going deeper into the reality of union with God.

In my own denomination (Lutheran), where grace is held to be at the center of Christian doctrine (where it belongs when considering access to

---

41. 2 Cor 5:19.

42. Rom 8:2.

43. Rom 6:3–11.

44. 1 Cor 1:30.

45. Gal 2:16 (CEB). For a discussion of the translation "faithfulness of Christ" rather than "faith in Christ" see Hays, *Faith of Jesus Christ*. For its significance, see Wright, *Justification*.

46. 2 Cor 3:18.

the presence and power of God), the focus often moves little beyond God's acceptance. Being received into a life of transformation is often given short shrift. Richard Rohr quotes Luther when he says that "the best that Luther could do was offer what he said was 'a layer of snow over a pile of manure.'" In my mind, Rohr has provided a caricature of a form of Lutheran confessional theology that has given little place for real transformation or in Rohr's discussion, divinization.[47] Luther himself wrote of human transformation: "Faith is a work of God in us, which changes us and brings us to birth anew from God (cf. John 1). It kills the old Adam, makes us completely different people in heart, mind, senses, and all our powers, and brings the Holy Spirit with it."[48]

We see the power for change outward to others "in Christ." Our relationships and communal reality are transformed by becoming one body *in Christ* and, individually members one of another.[49] In Christ, the dividing walls of hostility come down. Partnerships are formed across social divisions of class, ethnicity and gender.[50] What makes for status in a hierarchical world finds no foothold "in Christ." It is the being in Christ and growing in Christ that brings tangible, concrete change. As we went through spiritual change at St. Thomas, experiencing the welcome of Christ, we saw our congregation increasingly becoming economically diverse. What had been a relatively middle-class congregation came to span a range of diversity from homeless to professional, poor to affluent, all learning to welcome one another with the welcome of Christ, which meant being responsive to each other's needs.

This participation in Christ is, at the same time, participation in the divine nature. We are, as Eastern Christianity emphasizes and Western Christianity recognizes, deified. We are becoming children of God through the Child of God. The change we undergo is one of gaining our true selves in union with God.[51] The reality of incarnation, God present in God's creation, embodied in humanity, is foundational for understanding human

47. Rohr, *Immortal Diamond*, 122.

48. Luther, *Preface to Romans*, para 15. Finnish theologians Mannermaa and Kärkkäinen have shown the importance of participation in Christ for Luther and its significance for human transformation: Mannermaa, *Christ Present in Faith*; Kärkkäinen, *One with God*.

49. Rom 12:5.

50. Gal 3:28.

51. Luther also writes of the grace of God deifying us (Kärkkäinen, *One with God*, 47).

beings, prior to any discussion of the condition of sin that makes the cross of Christ necessary. Growth as human beings, therefore, is always growth in union with God by grace, as a gift in which we participate. While it is by the grace of God that we come to realize ourselves in God through Christ, we nevertheless *participate* in this reality. Our desire, seeking, and openness, as well as turning, surrendering, trusting, deciding, and acting involve us in this growth of our true selves in God. But, of course, always by God's grace.

I lift up this central reality of participation in Christ as union with God, because all true change begins here. The movement outward of our congregations for the sake of others, for their true liberation into who God intends them to be, begins here. Consequently, the word of God is always, in some manner, a call back to God and to our true selves. Paul's "now is the day of salvation" is for every day; salvation is always union with God. Everything else flows from this.

Simply talking about God's acceptance as if it were nothing more than letting us off the hook for something we feel guilty about or providing us with an imputed righteousness that leaves us unchanged, will only hinder us from the transformation we must undergo. The world needs congregations of people who are being changed, and therefore becoming children of God and therefore "salt, light, and yeast," manifesting the grace and love of God. If we are, before the world, merely religious organizations, defined as such because we observe various rituals and confessions as add-ons to our already self-predetermined busy lives, then we have little to offer other than what is offered outside the walls of our churches.

The hard words and difficult life of Jesus must be kept before us with the call to enter into this life. Do what he says. Grow in walking his walk. "Whoever says, 'I abide in him,' ought to walk just as he walked."[52] This becomes possible for us because he is the Christ, and we have entrance into Christ as a gift from God. In Christ, we are made alive to God and alive to others to serve them, not out of fear, guilt, or duty, but from the love of God poured into our hearts by the Spirit.[53]

All we need for the transformation of our churches is "in Christ Jesus" universally present and available, concretely providing our call and action. Our praxis is in Christ Jesus. This, of course, means a very particular way of life: one of envisioning and acting. Those who pay attention to the hard words of Jesus (hard, because of their truth) will readily recognize false

52. 1 John 2:6.
53. Rom 5:5.

claimants to being "church." The so-called prosperity gospel, particularly in its more extreme forms, puts a Christian mask upon its idolatry of health, wealth, and wisdom. Moralistic (and legalistic) religion masks an idolatry of self-made righteousness that allows us to judge others. Fundamentalist religion, particularly in its fundamentalist element, masks the idolatry of self-made security in rigid doctrinal structures that guard against reality (for example, finding ever more convoluted ways to argue against biological evolution).

My concern, however, is especially with historic, "mainline" churches, in the Western tradition—the tradition with which I am most familiar (although I believe Eastern churches also will recognize themselves here). These are churches that have "been there, done that." They have a history that forms a broad experience which continues to be drawn from. That history reminds them, at times, of pitfalls *before* they are overlooked and stumbled into. There is often a wealth of wisdom and a depth of experience encapsulated in their traditions and confessions. But many of them are like sleeping giants. There is great potential in them for initiating change in society, but they are either asleep or only half awake. They need an awakening or even a resurrection.

They must come back to their roots in Jesus Christ, not as a doctrinal position, but as the experience of dying and rising. It is our experience that must be attended to, not simply more confessional education. Those who are pastors and leaders in the church must see themselves as ambassadors of reconciliation to God, at a fundamental level. God chooses to make God's appeal through us; so we must, as Paul did, entreat others "on behalf of Christ" to "be reconciled to God."[54] I can hear Jesus' words in this entreaty: "Repent and believe for the reign of God is at hand." Now is the time! I recall many years ago being in a Roman Catholic church that was undergoing a spiritual renewal. Across the front of the church, from one side to the other, hung a giant banner that read, "Be reconciled to God." The people who gather in our churches, who come for many different reasons and with their many idolatries, must hear—as we all must—the clear call to reconciliation with God. It is the basis for real change in our lives.

It is very easy to become comfortable with our confessions, even smug in our present praxis, carrying within us the assumption that we are not so distant from the reality of being in God. When we hear the words "be reconciled to God" addressing us, we may find ourselves disturbed, for the

54. 2 Cor 5:18–21.

words imply that we need to be reconciled, that the relationship is broken, that we are alienated. When we acknowledge this condition, however, we are better able to hear the good news: God is in Christ bringing us back to God—and to our true selves. In this message, we hear God's welcome and acceptance. But, we also hear that this acceptance is meant to lead us to a turning of our lives over to God. God's acceptance must not be taken for granted, for it means that the way is open to come back. Turn from false attachments. Come to God. Grow in union with God, for that is reconciliation.

Only this movement into God is at the same time truly a movement outward, as salt, light and yeast in the world, for we are being freed from false dependencies that have had us bound inward, bent in upon ourselves—false selves of our own making, as we have attempted to gain our lives in and of ourselves without God. We have to be released outward. Consequently, pastors and leaders must attend to the spiritual dynamics of those in their charge and therefore must exercise spiritual discernment. The hermeneutical move from exegesis to the "thus says the Lord" is a spiritual dynamic.

The point is this: As important as are exegesis and theological knowledge, they do not by themselves address the spiritual realities of the people we serve. It is not enough to pass on a kind of textbook knowledge of our confessions, so that members learn how to talk (in my denomination) Lutheran. Gaining theological knowledge does not by itself enable individuals to draw closer to God, or to make decisions about particular situations or their callings, just as practical theology is not simply an application of theoretical theology, but involves a way of perceiving in its own right. An inescapable spiritual element is involved when, moving outward, we make decisions and choose a course of action that often has us wrestling with false spirits, idols, and obsessions.

3

Entrenched

In my early years at St. Thomas, the church council decided to install a wrought iron fence across the front of the courtyard. Our church building formed a U shape with one side as the sanctuary, the other side the parish house and, at the bottom of the U, the fellowship hall. The courtyard was the inner space created by these buildings and it opened out to the street. The erected fence closed off the courtyard from the street. It secured the windows within the courtyard from break-ins (of which we had some experience). It also prevented people from the street entering into the sanctuary of the courtyard with its garden and shade tree and benches, closing it off to homeless people who might venture into the space for the night. Our space was secured and we had found another way to wall ourselves off from the world to which Jesus sent us.

We were unable to see this, however. Our attachment to our security had us bound. It provided the parameters of our vision. It made our decision to install a fence seem entirely reasonable. In order to see differently, we would have to acknowledge our addiction to our security and by the grace of God be released outward.

God's liberating work did open our hearts, and a few years after erecting the fence, we invited our neighborhood to a series of outside gatherings every Wednesday, Thursday and Friday evening in August. We provided a barbecue and food in front of our church and brought our worship and prayer ministry out into the courtyard. The fence was in the way, and we took it down.

Addiction

An early meaning of the word "addict" according to the Merriam-Webster dictionary was "to attach (oneself) as a follower to a person or adherent to a cause," so that a person could say, "we sincerely addict ourselves to Almighty God." In other words, we attach ourselves to God; we depend upon God. Now, this is not the way we use this word currently, but it helps us to understand something about addiction. If we are not addicted to God in the above sense of dependence, we will be addicted to something else.

Addiction has to do with attachment; it has to do with being dependent or stuck on something other than the true source of our lives. Spiritually speaking, it is closely related to idolatry, which is the worship of (or addiction to) ourselves or some aspect of ourselves. Our lives become wrapped around our idols. We are attached to them and serve them, and they have us bound and hurting. I have heard recovering drug addicts refer to their drug of choice as simultaneously their best friend and their worst enemy. They could not live without it and it was killing them. It is said that addiction is a disease and, indeed, it is. But at its center, it is a *spiritual* disease that can only be truly healed through a spiritual program and journey.

In many respects, the spiritual turn outward at St. Thomas started with the experience of recovering drug addicts in our congregation, who were testifying to the grace and power of God that was setting them free. They gave witness to the work of God in what they were experiencing. As they continued their spiritual journeys, they recognized addictions beyond addictions to drugs. Others who did not struggle with drug addiction realized they were facing other kinds of addictions, and reached out to God for help and mercy.

Often, when we come to address the addiction that is at the forefront of our lives and we experience liberation, other addictions come to light. Our addictions or idols are interconnected. There is something like a "council of gods." Martin Luther King made the connection in his "Beyond Vietnam" speech at Riverside Church in New York in 1967; he connected racism with other idols that effected our involvement in the Vietnam War. Racism, militarism, materialism, capitalism, and greed formed an alliance.

People get stuck on—addicted to—all kinds of things: food, sugar, caffeine, chocolate, clothes, social media, technology, television, shopping malls, online shopping, and jewelry. We can be addicted to money and power, control and security, sex and pleasure, work and achievement, other people's approval and acceptance, emotions and attitudes. We can be addicted to an ethnic group ("our people"), our nation, guns, military power, righteousness (ours), religion, the Bible, and so on. Anything and any aspect of our lives can become an addiction. If what we are addicted to is taken away from us, we go through withdrawal symptoms. We crave it, sometimes as if our life depended upon it. At the least, removing what we are addicted to makes us depressed.

Some people talk as if some addictions are good addictions; for example, "I am addicted to health foods (or to running or exercise)." But no addiction is good for us, because what we are addicted to, dependent on, or feel we cannot live without—when ultimately it is God we cannot live without—gets in the way of our experiencing the goodness and power and peace of God. We were created for attachment to God. When we are "addicted" to God, in love with God, we are free with a freedom to love in an outward movement to others.

The reason Jesus' message included repentance (as did the prophets before him) is because it is necessary to turn away from that which already reigns in our lives to receive God's reign. Under the reign of love—for God is love—we are truly free. Paul continued the proclamation of this message. It is interesting to note that in perhaps the earliest of Paul's letters, 1 Thessalonians, it is clear from his reference to the Thessalonians' response to his message that he called them to turn "to God from idols."[1] His message concerning "justification by faith" came later, in reaction to those who would put faith in themselves (and their works) rather than or in addition to God—an idolatrous stance. As such, the issue of justification was related to the foundational message of repentance and faith in God.

The turning is necessary for our freedom to love and for our release outward. What becomes clear about addictions, obsessions, and idolatries, when we attempt to rid ourselves of them, is that they have our wills bound. We are entrenched, caught up in, overtaken, and made captive, and cannot free ourselves. It is at this point, where we realize our bondage, that we may find ourselves on our knees crying out to God. We discover grace; we discover, in our weakness, God's strength.

At times, drug addicts would share with me their herculean struggle with the third step in the twelve-step program. This third step has to do with making "a decision to turn our will and our lives over to the care of God, as we understood God." Some would tell me that they do not want this drug addiction anymore—that they have turned it over to God, but are

1. 1 Thess 1:9–10.

still held captive. I would tell them that it was not enough to turn over their addiction (which they no longer wanted) to God, but they would have to turn their wills and lives (which they *did* want) over to God. At that point, we were talking about the *real* struggle and decision which was impossible without God. They would feel their powerlessness and I would give them Jesus' directions, "Ask, and it will be given you; search, and you will find; knock, and the door will be opened for you. For everyone who asks receives, and everyone who searches finds, and for everyone who knocks, the door will be opened."[2] I would encourage them to bring their helplessness to God and ask God to do for them what they have been unable to do for themselves: to surrender their lives to God. (In Christ, who surrendered himself to God's will even to the point of dying on a cross, we experience surrender.)

We are all addicts and idolaters and must all take the third step; and we all need God's grace to do that. We can hardly help others with this step unless we take it for ourselves (and continue to take it). Pastors and leaders in the church are under call to proclaim this step of repentance and faith to people who, like ourselves, are entrenched, addicted and bound. We have to speak concretely to the addictions that are present among the people we serve. We have to name the idols. Sometimes we must take symbolic action, as Jesus did when he overturned the tables of the money changers in the temple. Some pastors have removed the American flag from the sanctuary, where it stood at the side of the altar of the one God. They then had to address the idolatry that the reaction to this action made apparent. They had to speak the truth in love.

We often deal with particular idols of individuals—the ones that have been at the forefront of their lives, getting in the way of their relationships, robbing them of joy, entrenching them in habitual inaction in the face of the obvious needs of others and themselves. We have to name these idols; we must place them up front so that first steps can be taken, so that each of us can admit that we are powerless over these attachments and acknowledge that they make our lives unmanageable, for they keep us from God's will and call.

Comfort and convenience, for example, are major idols in American society. We bow down to our comfort zones and make choices on the basis of whether or not we will be inconvenienced. We avoid taking up our cross to follow. When we truly begin to address this condition, we find ourselves

2. Matt 7:7–8.

helpless and in need of God's grace, which alone can set us free. In fact, the call to deny ourselves and take up our cross, when clearly proclaimed and truly heard, positions our idols of comfort and convenience before us in a way that cannot be ignored. In our desire to follow Jesus, we have to admit our powerlessness over that which would keep us from our calling; we must come in our weakness to the one who is our strength. What we are describing here is the way of dying and rising which is ours in Christ Jesus. We have to turn from—that is, let go or die to—false attachments, so that we may come alive to God and God's purposes.

No church programming based on organizational principles taken from insights of the corporate world will help us here, nor will the many studies done and statistics gathered on "successful" churches. Demographics and social trends will not help here. They certainly may help with some institutional operations, but not with the dying and rising, the admitting (getting past denial) and the surrendering. These are the fundamental spiritual realities of being the church, without which a church is a church in name only, remaining turned in upon itself, maintaining its traditions, as a world in need of good news is ignored.

I have used addiction as a way to talk about idolatry and in so doing have made idolatry analogous to a disease. But it is a disease that, unlike that which is initiated by airborne bacteria, involves our own decisions. With drug addiction, for example, we have to choose at some point to start taking drugs. I have mentioned racism as an idolatry and addiction. As such, it carries both that sense of disease—of being able to be caught like a cold, as a reality that is inherent to our environment—and a choice we make. Someone likened racism to a car out of control. We, who have our hands on the wheel, are being pushed and pulled and overwhelmed by the forces of racism that surround us. And yet, we cannot truthfully say that choice is not involved. Our hands on the wheel are not putting up the fight for control we would like to assume that they are. We who are white cling to the socially privileged positions that systemic racism has given us. Our denial is an element of that clinging.

Our disease is ultimately spiritual and therefore involves our will. It is for that reason we must confess, in the words of an Ash Wednesday liturgy, "It is by our fault, our most grievous fault." There do seem to be degrees of responsibility, however. A drug addict was much more capable of saying "no" to taking into his or her system a mind-altering drug, when first given the choice, than after a period of time during which physical, emotional, and mental dependence took over. And there are experiences in which we get caught up and that bring forth our reactions, but which we do not initiate. When sinned against, when the decisions and actions of others hurt, maim, and traumatize, we generally resort to whatever survival techniques suggest themselves, many of which—if maintained long term—are counter-productive and unhealthy for ourselves and others. Our reaction, stress, anxiety and hurt bring us to a place where we are already dying, already turning, like Israel exiled and held captive in Babylon. All the props have been knocked out from under us, and we are flat on our backs, looking up. Previously, when Israel was at ease in Zion and, in the words of Ezekiel, were like their sister Sodom who "had pride, excess of food, and prosperous ease, but did not aid the poor and needy," Ezekiel was given a message of repentance to proclaim: "Therefore say to the house of Israel, Thus says the Lord God: Repent and turn away from your idols."[3] Now, in exile, Israel, stripped of its false dependencies and held captive, is likened to a valley of dry bones: "Thus says the Lord God to these bones: I will cause breath to enter you, and you shall live. I will lay sinews on you, and will cause flesh to come upon you, and cover you with skin, and put breath in you, and you shall live; and you shall know that I am the Lord."[4] Whereas the previous message, addressing an arrogant people, was one of repentance; now, to a nation in captivity, the word is one of deliverance.

Addicts come for help when the pain gets great enough. They are ripe for change. Those who have suffered abuse and live with fear reach out for help. A woman came to St. Thomas who, in first meeting me following a worship service, immediately talked about help with preparing her funeral. It was a strange beginning. I wondered if she had a terminal illness. But I then learned that she was in an abusive relationship, filled with low-self-esteem and despair. She was reaching out—and members of the community became a support team for her, as she made the move out of her current situation into a healthy environment. Consider how Jesus responded to those who had been beaten down and were bound. He did not add extra burdens and condemnations, but brought release and healing. To the Pharisees, however, whose bondage lay in their play-acting and refusal to recognize what God was doing, Jesus declared their condition: "You whitewashed tombs!"[5] Pastors and leaders must exercise discernment

3. Ezek 16:49, 14:6.
4. Ezek 37:5–6.
5. Matt 23:27.

when it comes to declaring the word. To a people at ease, self-satisfied and self-righteous, speaking a simple word of God's acceptance and salvation without the call to change is much like the glib manner in which almost every politician mouths the words "God bless America." We are not called to issue blanket blessings over each others' lifestyles. On the other hand, those who have been beaten down, whether by their own decisions or the oppressive actions of others, do not need us to cast further judgments upon them. They need to hear the word of deliverance and healing. To the man oppressed by the devil, beset by a legion of evil spirits, overwhelmed and out of his mind, for whom the word of repentance—in that moment—held little meaning, Jesus said, "Come out of the man, you unclean spirit!"[6] With a command exercised under the power of the Spirit, the man was released.

For some years at St. Thomas, early on, I kept up a theme that contrasted a social club church turned in on itself with the community of Jesus' followers. Along with this theme was the message, "For those who want to save their life will lose it, and those who lose their life for my sake will save it."[7] If we seek to save and secure our fellowship, we will lose it. On the other hand, if we lose our lives for the sake of the world around us, for the sake of the gospel going out to that world, we will be secured in Christ and in Christ's mission. At times, I found I had to do as the prophet in Isaiah 50, "set my face like flint" and keep proclaiming the message. But as we underwent a transformation into a community of Jesus' followers, the theme changed. Now, the message was much more that of addressing broken, needy people, both those who, by God's grace, were undergoing the change from a club church and those who were being drawn into what was increasingly a fellowship of broken people experiencing God's liberation and healing. At times, the word is a "John the Baptist message" of repentance. At other times, it is a setting forth the image of Christ's outstretched hands upon the cross, revealing the welcome of God to hurting, pressed down and addicted people.

Our addictions have turned us away from one another and created division. It is God's deliverance that truly forms a community of broken people experiencing God's grace.

6. Mark 5:8.
7. Luke 9:24.

Addiction and the Other

In the twelve-step program of Alcoholics Anonymous, eight of the last nine steps have to do with our relationship to others. After acknowledging that our lives have become unmanageable, believing that God can restore us to sanity, and deciding to turn our will and lives over to the care of God, we are given eight steps that have to do with others in our lives. These include: a searching and fearless moral inventory of ourselves; admitting to God, to ourselves and to another human being the exact nature of our wrongs; being ready to have God remove all these defects of character; humbly asking God to remove our shortcomings; and making a list of all persons we had harmed, becoming willing to make amends to all.

These are powerful steps into new life. It is in the nature of addictions to have us blaming others and excusing our own failings. These steps require us to attend to our own motives and behavior. Our inability to see the humanity of others, and our tendency to make them other than us, is an outcome of our false attachments and our being turned in upon ourselves. When others' lives and expressions of themselves do not align with our sensibilities, perspectives, and values, we write them off. On the basis of our false dependencies, we dismiss others. They are not like us in their humanity (and we are far from our true humanity).

This is manifested whenever we talk about people as other than us; for example, whenever those of us who are white say, "Black people need to do something about violence in their communities." Why don't we say, "*We* need to understand and give support to addressing the problems in *our* urban centers"? How did black people become "not us?" If it were not for the addiction of racism, we would talk and act differently. We would recognize our common humanity, our relatedness, our history of violence (the brutality of slavery and its legacy). If we saw ourselves as kin, we would know something of the valiant work that is being done to address poverty and violence in communities that may be distant from our own. If I have family living in a difficult or dangerous environment, I tend to get to know their situation—what they face and its causes.

When we do not experience ourselves as part of one family and one human race, we say, "What is wrong with these people?"—revealing our inordinate lack of self-awareness. We make generalizations related to ethnicity, nationality, class, gender, sexual orientation, political party, and religion in order to dismiss others from our common humanity and free ourselves to talk about them, to blame them for *our* troubles and to excuse our own sin. In the process, we are robbed of compassion and mercy. Our prejudices and fears then make us vulnerable to being manipulated by those who would use us (gain our support or votes) by appealing to these prejudices.

We are entrenched in our "otherizing" and not particularly open to reason. There needs to be a spiritual liberation that includes "a searching and fearless moral inventory of ourselves." The first step, however, is to *acknowledge* our addictions and idols. For most of us, this is not an easy step. We get touchy about our idols and our addictions (when we are in denial about them). If someone points them out, there is often conflict.

Conflict

A new member came to me with concerns about a drinking problem. His admission was not a surprise; the signs of alcoholism had already surfaced. Yet when I suggested that he go to an agency in the community for an assessment regarding alcoholism, he was deeply offended. This was a remarkable reaction in a congregation with a ministry to addicts and with a number of recovering addicts among its members—a congregation that regularly celebrated members' clean time. He had come to me for counsel concerning something that he realized was becoming a problem, but when the possible addiction was actually named, he took offense.

A number of years ago at a conference gathering of churches in Chicago, at which there was about an equal mixture of white people and black people, a preacher illustrated what true inclusion might look like by lifting up various national symbols. These were symbols that were deeply rooted in the beginnings of a nation anchored in white supremacy. African-Americans had no part in the formation of these symbols. So, this pastor imagined what it would be like to take a fresh look at these symbols and make them more inclusive. He named about four symbols; I recall his talking about adding some green and black to the American flag. What was striking was the reaction to this simple illustration. African-Americans embraced the signs of inclusion in these symbols with joy, while tension increasingly grew among those who were white, as their symbols were being altered in this imaginative exercise. We get touchy about our idols.

We should not be surprised, therefore, at the tension and conflict that are produced when we name and unmask the idols of those gathered in our churches. And naming the idols we must do! After all, how else are we going to call people to "turn to God from idols, to serve a living and true

God"? Of course, we are not to do this as their judges, but as those who, as idolaters, stand under the same word. We are to speak the truth in love. Even so, there will be some who will respond like the rich young man who walked away from Jesus, sad because he was, at that point, unwilling to depart from his idol. There will be others who will fight the naming of idols. It is not the kind of church they want. They will, in one way or another, work against change and find others sympathetic to their ends. We should not be surprised or alarmed by the conflict.

Others, however, will respond, with the help of the Spirit, by turning to God and away from the idols that are being named and from which they are being set free. They will rejoice in the gift of freedom as children of God and give thanks for God's compassion and mercy. They will find themselves being freed to love one another and to move beyond the walls of the church building. By grace they are being liberated through faith; and they realize this is not their own doing, but is the gift of God.[8]

During the years at St. Thomas, when the vision of a community of Jesus' followers was being lifted up over against an inturned club church, there was increased division. There were those who were "getting it," who were coming to understand what it meant to be the people of God with a mission and who were desirous of living out that reality by God's grace. On the other hand, there were those who seemed committed to *our* place, *our* building, *our* people, *our* control. I began to understand Paul's word: "I hear that there are divisions among you; and to some extent I believe it. Indeed, there have to be factions among you, for only so will it become clear who among you are genuine."[9] We were, in fact, gaining clarity about being Jesus' followers; it was being increasingly modeled so that others could see, even while there was conflict over the direction of the church.

We can get side-tracked by conflict or we can recognize it as part of the growing pains, part of the spiritual journey. It exists, but does not always need to be addressed. Jesus spent most of his time mentoring his disciples and responding to the needs of those who came to him for healing and deliverance. He chose when and how to address those who were in conflict with him. He was particularly concerned about their effect on others:

> Then Jesus said to the crowds and to his disciples, "The scribes and the Pharisees sit on Moses' seat; therefore, do whatever they teach you and follow it; but do not do as they do, for they do not practice

8. Eph 2:8.
9. 1 Cor 11:18–19.

what they teach. They tie up heavy burdens, hard to bear, and lay them on the shoulders of others; but they themselves are unwilling to lift a finger to move them."[10]

At times, the conflicts must be addressed, particularly as they bring harm to others. But our fundamental calling is to nurture those who are responding to the call of God and respond to those who are in need. Disciples must be mentored and encouraged. Attention must be given to the growth of ministry as God's people discover their gifts and learn to discern how God would have them use their gifts.

Above all, we must not shy away from naming the idols, proclaiming God's liberation from addictions and the effects of past hurts and from all that would hold us in bondage, and then calling for response. Extend Jesus' invitation, "Come to me, all you that are weary and are carrying heavy burdens, and I will give you rest."[11]

How we recognize and address addictions is related to the environment in which they are exercised. We must pay attention to the context of our addictions and their affects.

Context

The impact of our addictions is experienced individually and locally as well as nationally and globally. Addictions to our own pleasure (and the avoidance of pain, including the pain of others), and having to be in control immediately affect our relationships with family and friends. For other addictions, however, the impact may not be personally recognized. My addiction to security when it focuses on my nation's security may affect people in other places remote from myself as I (and others) are willing to put up with violence and loss of life at a distance, if it means I will feel more secure. If I am white and my family and friends are white, my racism may not, at first glance, seem to readily affect my personal relationships. But it *will* affect others, particularly as my feelings are expressed at the ballot box in terms of the kind of government I want—a government that I believe will serve people like me (and, without acknowledging it, maintain a white supremacy in this nation). For example, Donald Trump was largely a white people's choice, elected by a majority of white people significant enough

10. Matt 23:1–4.
11. Matt 11:28.

to overcome the votes of people of color. His utter lack of qualifications and temperament for the office were simply ignored because of underlying—and unacknowledged—racism, which, as with all addictions, makes our lives unmanageable, subjecting us to very bad choices.

At one time, the gathering space for the African-American congregation that I served for almost three decades on Chicago's south side provided a place for a white congregation. When African-Americans moved into what was then a white neighborhood and reached a particular percentage of the population, whites moved out very quickly in what has been called "white flight"—a dynamic that has been played out in neighborhood after neighborhood. However this flight might be analyzed, at the root is racism. Its effects are many and include the redlining of neighborhoods by banks or banks moving out with the consequent breakdown of the local economy.

There is another outcome, however, that has generally been ignored. As congregations in these neighborhoods lost members in the flight to the suburbs, suburban churches gained members. But they did not gain members by the power of the gospel, but by the power of fear. And the congregations that grew from this influx often had the appearance of thriving, even as they remained bound by addictions and idolatries that had motivated their actions. If those addictions were addressed with the gospel of liberation, I would imagine at least some people moving back to neighborhoods from which they had run, now being energized by the power of that gospel.

Paul writes of the "message of the gospel" that came to the Thessalonian church "not in word only, but also in power and in the Holy Spirit and with full conviction." They received this word "in spite of persecution" and "with joy inspired by the Holy Spirit," so that "the word of the Lord has sounded forth" from them to the surrounding regions.[12] The gospel had released them outward to others.

We are called to declare the same gospel of God's reign, which is near and, even right now, can release us from addictions and idolatries. Therefore, with Jesus (and Paul) we learn to say, "repent, and believe in the good news."[13] We proclaim, "God's welcome and forgiveness and transformation are present for us, therefore turn and receive. Do not stay stuck and bound, but receive your liberation." We proclaim a gospel of liberation, not only from guilt (a focus of the Reformation), but from all forms of bondage,

12. 1 Thess 1:4–6.
13. Mark 1:15.

oppression, and oppressive ways, that we may be freed to do justice, love mercy, and walk humbly with God.

Pastors and leaders in the church must widen the context of the message beyond local situations by widening the circle of those to whom we listen. This is particularly true for addressing racism in these United States of America. Its subtle, deceptive nature must not deter us. We, who are white, must acknowledge our racism, going ever deeper in understanding it, listening to the cries of those who are affected by it, being led by leaders and pastors of color. We must humble ourselves and draw into the light of God as it shines through our brothers and sisters of color in the body of Christ, allowing our white privilege and euro-centric ways to be unmasked.

Reggie Williams writes in *Bonhoeffer's Black Jesus* that "imperialist loyalties to nation and *Volk* became synonymous with claims to Christ-centeredness for many Christians in Germany" in the years leading up to the Nazi government.[14] It is interesting how easily nationalistic tendencies get collapsed into a "Christ-centeredness." Jesus says that we cannot serve two masters, but apparently we readily try, without realizing it. Bonhoeffer's growth as a follower of Jesus during his year in the United States was not related primarily to his studies at Union Seminary, but to his experience at Abyssinian Baptist Church in Harlem. It was there that his context for the lived faith was broadened, and he encountered a theology that rose in the crucible of suffering and oppression. He saw, from the underside of history, the effects of imperialism and colonialism. He was given a different vantage point from which to view that to which he had been blind.

Our Christ-centeredness, our experience of surrender to God, is experienced within the immediate contexts of the idols of which we are conscious. A drug addict makes a decision to turn his or her will and life over to the care of God and take steps on the road to recovery, experiencing new life and freedom with every day of sobriety. With growing clarity, the addict recognizes the extent to which addiction to drugs has taken over and laid claim to his or her life. At the same time there comes to be a growing awareness of other addictions, and the twelve-step spiritual journey continues. Spiritual growth involves a broadening context in which we are able to view idols we did not know we had. Others help us with that. The community of faith, local and global, with all its diversity of experience, helps us.

As with all addictions and idolatries, the first step is acknowledging, "admitting that we are powerless over our addiction, that our lives have

14. Williams, *Bonhoeffer's Black Jesus*, Chapter 2, Section 6.

become unmanageable." We cannot do that by ourselves. We need to undergo an intervention. This is true as we allow the context of our addictions to widen. Just as family and friends, in an intervention, gather around their loved one who is addicted and share the effects of their addiction on their lives, so we, who are white, must let our brothers and sisters who are affected by our racism and white privilege share with us the effects of that racism on their lives. How else can we come out of denial, acknowledge that we cannot manage our lives in relation to others, and turn our wills over to God? Our wills have been held by a white supremacist view that we have denied with all manner of face-saving mental deceptions. As we come into the light, with the help of God and others, we acknowledge and turn to God, who is our help. As we live into this process and journey, we do as the twelfth step directs us: "Having had a spiritual awakening as the result of these steps, we try to carry this message to others, and to practice these principles in all our affairs."

Continuing our reflection on the addiction of racism and expecting a growing number of recovering racists in our congregations as this addiction is addressed, its depths increasingly acknowledged and growing freedom experienced, we must encourage one another with the twelfth step, which has to do with praxis. We who are white must become allies in movements toward justice and liberation from oppressive ways and systems. Freed for action, we will have to commit ourselves to gaining knowledge, not only of our own personal and individual racism, but of institutional and systemic racism. We must then be engaged in working for change, knowing that the Spirit of God is our helper for discernment and resolve.

Similar observations can be made, of course, concerning classism, sexism, ageism, militarism, hedonism, materialism, and so on. Just as there are many aspects to our being entrenched, so there is an ever-widening experience of our liberation. As we are being liberated in ever more diverse ways, so does our ministry of liberation also widen.

4

Liberation

ADDICTS EXPERIENCE LIBERATION WHEN their wills are no longer held captive to a drug. A person whose life has been constricted by fear and held bound in an abusive relationship experiences liberation when empowered to step out of the relationship and enter a journey of healing. The person stressed by poverty, unable to provide for the needs of his or her family, experiences liberation when finally receiving a living wage. Those whose decisions and potential are limited by systemic racism experience liberation when there is social justice. The person who, burdened by guilt, experiences liberation when forgiven. Persons whose lives are focused on their own comfort and pleasure experience liberation when they are able to see the needs of others, and are free to respond with compassion and mercy. When we begin to experience release from a false self of our construction and find in God our true self, that is liberation.

Liberation takes many forms and always carries an ingredient of rescue. None of us are self-sufficient. We need rescue that comes from beyond our own effort. The person who experiences doors opened that had previously been closed because of systemic racism can be grateful for movements for change that instigated changes in laws, policies, and attitudes. The person no longer faced by decisions between health care and paying the rent, can be grateful for movements for a living wage and health care for all. The person liberated from an abusive relationship can be grateful for the help of others and for support systems. The person liberated from guilt can be grateful for the mercy of God and others. Recovering addicts—including those addicted to their comfort and pleasure—are grateful to their "higher power."

The good news is that there is rescue and liberation. The signs are all around us in word and action.

Freedom

"For freedom Christ has set us free."[1] The work of Christ is the work of liberation. The saving act of God through Christ Jesus is the act setting us free that we might live free.

In the context of his letter to the Galatians, Paul is referring to a freedom from attempting a self-made righteousness under the law, a righteousness that is impossible to produce. We are freed from the tyranny of striving to establish ourselves and our actions in and of ourselves, in our own strength. We are freed from that endeavor so that we may now be led by the Spirit. In other contexts, for Paul, deliverance in Christ means freedom from sin, the power of evil and the world. It is critical for us to see God's liberating work in its broadest dimensions. The freedom for which Christ has set free is broadened by contexts and issues beyond that of the Galatian churches' struggle with legalism.

In the article on "salvation" in the Interpreter's Dictionary of the Bible, published in 1962, a distinction is made between "secular" uses of the concept of deliverance (deliverance from adversity, oppression, captivity, death, disease) and "technical theological or specifically religious" uses (forgiveness and deliverance from sin). This is certainly a modern, post-enlightenment view that is far removed from the world of the Bible, and from a Christianity that finds its life and expression from following Jesus. Theology has been moving away from this view, but the old seeds sown continue to produce fruit in many congregations. This perspective remains one of the marks of the middle-class-values captivity of the church, where people learn to divide up their lives between the religious and secular. In so doing, they diminish the radical call of God and reduce the mission of the church to a private "religious" sphere—and leave other forms of liberation to conflicting "secular" ideologies.

Words like "salvation" and "redemption" have taken on a religious meaning, separated from much of our human experience. While they have become theological shorthand for how God deals with our sin as that

---

1. Gal 5:1.

which separates us from God, they have often been confined to a very narrow view of this work of God. Certainly, liberation from sin is a central issue, since it speaks to a fundamental spiritual entrenchment that keeps us from becoming who we are created to be. As individuals, our forgiveness and deliverance from false dependency frees us to be the people of God, released outward to serve others. We are delivered into ever-widening circles of compassion, into the liberating work of God that addresses the whole human condition. However, if our understanding of God's "salvation" tends narrowly to freedom from guilt (forgiveness) and God's acceptance and "going to heaven when I die" without transformation, we will end up with an unreal and faithless salvation, with little in the way of outreach to others with a good news that speaks to every dimension of a person's life.

A brief consideration of how the notions of salvation and redemption are used in the Bible reveals what such a narrow view excludes. Hebrew and Greek words for salvation and redemption carry the sense of rescue, deliverance and restoration. "Redemption" also bears the meaning of a cost for deliverance (for example, the ransom price for a slave or captive), but in most contexts the emphasis is on deliverance itself rather than its cost. This is especially true in Second Isaiah[2] and Psalms, where God is our redeemer (or deliverer) from captivity (in Babylon), and from troubles, enemies, oppression, violence, and iniquities. God's liberating work covers a wide domain. The poor cry out to God, "As for me, I am poor and needy, but the Lord takes thought for me. You are my help and my deliverer; do not delay, O my God."[3] And those oppressed pray, "Contend, O Lord, with those who contend with me; fight against those who fight against me!"[4] And those in trouble, "Consider my affliction and my trouble, and forgive all my sins."[5]

In the Gospels, "redemption" and "salvation" are expressive of this tradition. Peter calls out to Jesus when he is afraid that he is about to drown and Jesus "saves" him. A prophet, Anna, "[spoke] about the child [Jesus] to all who were looking for the redemption of Jerusalem."[6] The hope for the redemption or deliverance of Jerusalem was grounded in Israel's deliverance

---

2. Biblical scholars divide the book of Isaiah into First, Second, and often Third Isaiah. The prophesies of Isaiah in the eighth century BCE form the first division. Second Isaiah is an anonymous prophet of the sixth century BCE.

3. Ps 40:17.

4. Ps 35:1.

5. Ps 25:18.

6. Luke 2:38.

from exile in Babylon and bondage in Egypt. Therefore, Israel was expecting a similar liberation in its own land, subjugated as it was to Rome. This form of deliverance, which we would tend to call political, is seen in other ways. Jesus shares in the Hebrew prophets' judgment of the rich who trample the poor, or priests and kings who act not as shepherds who bind up the wounds of the sheep, but who oppress and injure them. Jesus bears witness against leaders who add burdens to those who are already pressed down, and calls out the machinations of Herod and the self-deception and expediency of Pilate. In all these things, along with deliverance from guilt and sin, we see the liberating ways of God. The whole of God's liberating work flows from God's love.

The dominant notion of salvation in the Gospels and the New Testament, of course, is concerned with our relationship with God and God's creation. In Zacchaeus's encounter with Jesus, salvation describes what has happened to him in relation to God and to other human beings. When Zacchaeus says to Jesus, "Look, half of my possessions, Lord, I will give to the poor; and if I have defrauded anyone of anything, I will pay back four times as much," Jesus responds with, "Today salvation has come to this house." Salvation takes Zacchaeus up into the work of God's reign, which moves him outward to others. The experience of conversion is the experience of being redirected from our inturned condition to the outward service of others. As we see in Jesus, this outward movement includes a ministry of healing, deliverance from evil, words of encouragement and hope in the God of mercy. All who draw near to receive God's reign give witness to and resist all powers that come against God's reign and liberating governance.

There is no distinction between a secular deliverance and a technically religious one. All forms of liberation of God our deliverer are "technically" theological, and the subject of theology, especially practical theology, as it addresses the practical action that love demands in the present. More fundamentally, we expect Christ's community to experience these various dimensions of liberation and to be serving others from that experience.

The story of Jesus' ministry to a woman "caught in the very act of committing adultery" provides a beautiful example of God's liberating ministry, as exercised in multiple forms.[7] The scribes and Pharisees drag the adulterous woman into the streets and have her stand before them. I imagine these men with stones in their hands ready to carry out the punishment prescribed in the law of Moses, but they first use the situation to test Jesus.

7. John 8:3–11.

What does he have to say about operating according to the law? Jesus ignores their question. Whatever their designs, Jesus is about God's work of
liberation. And he does two things. He first addresses this woman's oppressors: "Let anyone among you who is without sin be the first to throw a stone
at her." One by one, they leave, so that Jesus is alone with the woman. She
acknowledges that those who had condemned her to death are no longer
present, and Jesus says to her, "Neither do I condemn you. Go your way,
and from now on do not sin again." Jesus' ministry here is twofold. He calls
out the oppressors, and he liberates the one bowed down, freeing her into
the life God has for her.

We who are followers of Jesus have the same ministry of liberation.
We must speak truth to the oppressive forces of our society (which means
we must gain holy clarity for ourselves). We must do it in the presence of
those who are being victimized, so that they also can receive clarity about
their situation and not be taken in by the lies of those oppressing them. In
fact, at times we must do this first. Then we can personally attend to the
very real needs of the individual under fire and condemnation. We can
speak God's liberating word of forgiveness, welcome and new life, deliverance from sin, and the effects of the sins of others.

Liberation and the Church's Mission

With spiritual liberation and the re-centering of our lives, comes ever-
widening circles of liberation. We are released outward as we experience
freedom from false dependencies, lose our lives to God and others, experience healing of past hurts through forgiving others, and find our needs
being met within a loving community. As we experience release from fear
and anxiety into a trusting relationship with God, we no longer have to
avoid or run from the suffering of ourselves or others, but are being freed
to "take up our cross," to enter into the hurts and brokenness of our world.
We are being freed, not only to see the needs of others, but to respond with
a sense of calling. And we are grateful for having a calling and a purpose.

We may find ourselves praying for the children in our congregation
and neighborhood and then volunteering to tutor children in our congregation's after-school program. This was the journey for some members at
St. Thomas, who sensed a call to work with children. In the process, they
also saw what was lacking in the children's education and the inequity in
funding of inner-city schools in a state where schools were predominantly

supported by property taxes. This meant that rich areas had rich schools and poor areas had poor schools. Our children needed the liberation of our time, so they could receive tutoring. They also needed the liberation of social structures from the racism and classism that does not see or care about all children and that prevents them from having the education needed for their growth and achievement. The circle of liberation widened as we joined with others in a faith-based community organization to work for change in the way schools were funded in our state. We sought to liberate school funding from values and prejudices that excluded our students from the education needed to achieve their callings within American society.

Our witness took on a prophetic element as we witnessed to values that come from God's governance, in which focused attention is given to the least of these his children: the needy and pushed-aside. Our call was to a ministry of liberation from oppressive ways that diminished the God-given importance and giftedness of our children. At the same time, in keeping with community organizing principles, we sought to get achievable legislation passed that would make a difference in the lives of our children. In the face of entrenched injustice, we find that we must continue to speak the prophetic word:

> Woe to those who make unjust laws,
> to those who issue oppressive decrees,
> to deprive the poor of their rights
> and withhold justice from the oppressed of my people.[8]

The widening circles of liberation move out from spiritual conversion and personal healing to individual ministry (often with family and the family of God), to serving the stranger by sharing the "gospel of God [and] our own selves"[9] (Paul), to prophetic witness and action directed to what Martin Luther King Jr. called "the beloved community."[10] King considered it achievable that just laws could be passed and that just government policies could be implemented. He was convinced that even attitudes could change among diverse groups toward each other—although not without struggle. No change happens without struggle.

The continued widening of our liberating activity begins with the spiritual change that only happens by the grace of God. Until we begin to be

8. Isa 10:1–2 (NIV).

9. 1 Thess 2:8.

10. See Smith and Zepp, *Search for the Beloved Community*, 129–56.

liberated from our false dependencies, no amount of consciousness-raising or practical theologizing will get us there. Many of us are in denominations that excel in studying the problem, but remain distant from the activity and struggle necessary for real change. This is true for congregations as well. Many years ago, I interned in a very large and prestigious downtown congregation with a very active social justice committee—active, that is, in *discussing* the problems. Next to the church was a dilapidated building in which a half dozen men with addiction problems resided. I brought one of these men to Sunday School, and the members, while trying to be welcoming, were clearly uncomfortable and at a loss as to what to do. More study would not have helped them. Until we are released from false attachments, including the attachment to ourselves, to a false self (one we have structured apart from God), and the distance is closed between ourselves and others, more information will not help us.[11] Liberated by God into becoming our true selves that come from God, coming to know ourselves as radically needy for God, we can then see ourselves in others, whoever they are. We come to see that, in words attributed to Martin Luther, "We are all beggars."

One of the things that, at times, has been dramatically apparent with recovering addicts and victims of abuse who are experiencing emotional and spiritual healing is the degree to which new vistas are opened for action by the path of recovery. I think of recovering addicts at St. Thomas, who very quickly moved into acts of service in the congregation and participation in actions and demonstrations with the faith-based community organization with which we were involved. Recovering addicts were "set free" from a life-consuming attachment that radically restricted their horizons for action. I would hear recovering addicts say things like "I see trees today that I wasn't seeing before" or "I see beauty" or "I see the needs of my family that I had not been recognizing." Freed from one addiction, they were also able to see other false attachments and had a "spiritual program" to address them, and transformation continued. It was often not long before those recovering became involved in social justice actions.

There is a movement in the other direction as well—moving not so much from personal liberation to social justice action, but the other way around. There were some who, caring about issues facing our community, first became involved in the life of St. Thomas through working for social justice. Through such involvement, they had opportunity to sense the motivations of people of faith for this work, and through them God's liberating

11. For reflections on our structuring a false self, see Rohr, *Immortal Diamond*.

word, the kind that God speaks through Moses to Pharaoh: "Let my people go." Others were first involved at St. Thomas with serving in response to a neighborhood need, volunteering to tutor children in our after-school homework center. There they saw the love of God responding concretely to the needs of children and witnessed the closing prayer time, when children would make their various requests for prayer and have their needs acknowledged before God. The whole spectrum of God's liberating work gives witness to God—and that witness draws others in toward the center.

Liberation and Politics

Perhaps the most difficult word for many pastors and leaders of historic mainline churches to speak is the word that addresses the concrete political realities facing us. This is especially true for leaders serving white middle-class congregations where many members tend to view the general system of government as more or less adequate, no matter what the differing ideologies are within the congregation. It is a different matter for congregations that come from those sectors of society that experience a persistent negative impact of government systems. With congregations whose members experience pernicious injustice, there is generally an expectation that there will be a word concerning the political dimensions of our situation. (In the African-American congregation I served, I spoke from the pulpit against both Iraq wars, among other "hot" issues facing our society.) We would expect that, for congregations experiencing liberation from middle-class values and submission to God's ways of governing, there would be a yearning for a word that addresses the actions of government from the vantage point of the reign of God. Certainly, there is a word of the Lord that addresses a nation considering war, or that speaks to a nation's relationship to refugees, its care of the "least" among us, its operation of a criminal justice system, or it's equity in funding education for children. God has a word directed to these quite specific decisions that have great impact upon nations and our global village. The God of the Hebrew prophets and the book of Revelation addresses the decisions of rulers and leaders and the effects of those decisions.

From the above, it ought to be clear that the issue, for those called to proclaim a word of the Lord, is not alignment with existing political ideologies or philosophies. God's governance critiques all ideologies and persists in calling us into a new reality and into radically new relationships that are the work of God. The task of proclaimers of the word of God is to call forth faithfulness to God's way of governing and to being witnesses to God's call to love one another in truth and therefore with justice. This word, when it is directed in a specific and timely manner to various powers and current realities, tends to uncover and disturb our false allegiances. We must often proclaim a word to people who have bifurcated their lives into religious and secular, which is a convenient subterfuge for maintaining a form of Christianity alongside middle-class values. Acknowledging this should not disengage us from our call to speak a clear word to the situations of our time, but rather to speak contextually, identifying the values that co-opt our ability to hear and follow Jesus. Following the disturbance that clear speech directed to specific issues may cause, we may find that God has given us an opportunity to follow up with the pastoral care of individual members!

Reinhold Niebuhr, in his book *Moral Man and Immoral Society*, reminds us of the distance between the personal morality that subsists within families and among friends and the morality of society in relation to other nations and peoples.[12] As individuals, we will allow for atrocities (we may call them "collateral damage") in our name, when they are the actions of our nation for the sake of our security—atrocities that we would not allow on a close personal level. The ethics of God's reign removes that distance: "Do to others as you would have them do to you"[13]; "Love your enemies and pray for those who persecute you."[14] God's reign of justice and mercy is radically counter-cultural and, for global power dynamics and sensibilities, counter-intuitive. Nevertheless, the people of God are called to be witnesses to God's reign and to speak from the love of God for humanity—and to do so regardless of the prevalent political "realism." This also is true with domestic politics, where there is a distance of priorities between my family, my community (and people), and other communities.

Illinois has one of the most inequitable systems in the nation as far as funding public schools is concerned. A report from the Center for American Progress places Illinois' public schools in the category of "savage inequalities," a term first used by Jonathan Kozol.[15] It is "characterized by affluent suburbs with big houses on tree-lined streets, palatial high schools, top-notch lacrosse and fencing teams, and elite orchestras contrasted with

12. Niebuhr, *Moral Man and Immoral Society*.

13. Luke 6:31.

14. Matt 5:44.

15. Kozol, *Savage Inequalities*.

nearby urban ghettos replete with overcrowded and crumbling schools, high crime and considerable dropout rates."[16] A system of funding weighted to property taxes has tended toward inequity in financing education. For decades there have been attempts at reforming school financing, including moving its funding from property taxes to state income taxes. The opposition to reform tends to originate from the fear of loss. One state senator declared of a recent reform bill that it was "stealing from the rich to give to the poor."[17] Reform, of course, does not necessarily mean bringing other schools down, but raising up those in need—however, the fear is there. But what if, in the face of fear, affluent suburban churches became champions of equity in funding? In the midst of neighbors fearful for what they might be losing (and to whom), Christians came to be known as those who, beyond their own narrow self-interest, witness to justice for those who are lacking basic educational resources. Imagine suburban and urban churches working together for a reform that many in suburban areas have resisted. For that to happen, pastors and leaders would have to speak a concrete word in the context of the racial and class dynamics of our society, directed to specific choices laid before people. Those churches that have been undergoing a spiritual liberation, and whose vision of liberation has been expanding, would be those most prepared to hear such messages. They would more likely see it as in keeping with the gospel of liberation, for "it is the power of God for liberation to everyone who has faith . . . for in it the righteousness of God is revealed through faith for faith."[18] People who are being freed from false dependencies (and middle-class values) by the power of God are, at the same time, gaining sight to recognize the righteousness and justice of God in the present moment.

The "revelation of Jesus Christ" given to John "on the island called Patmos" provides a mirror for those seeking to be faithful witnesses in our time. The message of this document is directed to seven churches in a province of the Roman Empire. With the promised coming of Christ to bring all things to a close in him as the backdrop, these churches are encouraged to be steadfast witnesses to the end, not compromising with the world. These oppressed churches are told in advance of coming tribulation and

16. Baker, "America's Most Financially Disadvantaged," 10–13.

17. Zumbach and Lafferty, "New School Funding," para 13. (More recently, in August 2017, a new school funding formula became law and is an advancement toward equitable funding.)

18. Rom 1:16–17.

persecution, and they receive a word that speaks directly to their situation, in language they understand. They know Rome to be the new Babylon who, like the old Babylon, makes captive God's people and whose emperor is a monster who does the bidding of Satan.

What is striking is that these Christians have, at least generally, a common politics. They are unable to participate with their compatriots in the public festivals and worship of the gods that are seen as essential to the health of the city. They are unable to offer proper allegiance to the emperor, who is worshiped as a son of God and savior. They are unable to engage in war and violence.[19] Their commitments set them apart—and for that they are misunderstood and persecuted. They do not join in the glorification of Rome and the emperor, which was the nationalism of their time. They operate like citizens of an alternate nation or kingdom. They gather in small flocks, households of God, and yet they view themselves as belonging to a kingdom that reigns over all and is forever. Christ who "freed [them] from [their] sins by his blood . . . made them to be a kingdom, priests serving his God and Father, to him be glory and dominion forever and ever."[20] As long as they are faithful to that vision and reality, they will stand over against the nationalism and self-glorification of their time. But they must remain faithful unto death; so the seven churches thus are warned against complacency and compromise. Perhaps the strongest warning is directed to the seventh church, the church in Laodicea:

> I know your works; you are neither cold nor hot. I wish that you were either cold or hot. So, because you are lukewarm, and neither cold nor hot, I am about to spit you out of my mouth.[21]

These words come from Christ, "the faithful and true witness." God continues to call God's church to faithful commitment and witness, a witness that includes addressing the social and political issues and decisions of our time. This faithful witness and "common politics" certainly does not exclude differing opinions, disagreements over strategy and policy, or debate over next steps. Positions change as further knowledge of situations grow. We each make decisions and plans based on that of which we are aware; we can never wait until all the "facts" are in. But we can expect for a servant church, growing in response to God's way of governing, that there would

19. See Sider, *Early Church on Killing.*
20. Rev 1:5–6.
21. Rev 3:15–16.

be common contours to our politics. We would expect a foundational understanding of the restorative nature of God's justice, and that what makes for peace would define us as a people of faith. God's liberating power frees us from the very addictions, prejudices, fears, and false attachments that would divide us from our common purpose as God's children to do justice, love mercy, and walk humbly with our God.

Some may claim that the seven churches addressed by the book of Revelation were pressed by the brutality of Rome to a common position, and that our situation differs. And it is true that we, who reside in America, do not necessarily face the same brutality from our nation as that of Christians in the Roman empire—but some do. When we, as a nation, drop bombs in raid after raid and, in so doing, maim, kill, and terrorize (think of the children) in the name of our security, it is hard to imagine that we, as a nation, are not experienced as terrorists to those on the receiving end. And within our borders, if we are without white privilege or class privilege, we have a very different experience of oppression from those *with* privileges. If we do carry socially contrived privileges, then we must, with Jesus, decide for solidarity with those who do not. We must unite with, and listen to, the oppressed and marginalized ("For you know the grace of our Lord Jesus Christ, that though he was rich, yet for your sake he became poor, so that by his poverty you might become rich"[22]). In the process, we discover our own poverty and begin to gain true perspective on the oppressive forces of our society. We then find it necessary to give witness in word and action to God's ways and governance, contending with social and political patterns and priorities. As we do so, we discover a common ground to our politics, similar to the experience of the early church.

But, of course, what we *actually* give witness to is rooted where our faith truly resides. When this faith is, as Martin Luther expresses it, "a living, unshakeable confidence in God's grace," we experience God's liberating power. This same faith, which is also a "living, creative, active, powerful thing," has us engaged in a ministry of liberation in ever-widening circles, from personal to political.[23]

Pastors and leaders in the church must proclaim this expansive liberating word of God's reign, speaking the truth in love to the events and decisions of our nation and the world. We must do so against the backdrop of Christ's appearing, the anticipation of human history realizing its end in

22. 2 Cor 8:9.

23. Luther, *Preface to Romans*, paras 15–16.

the fullness of God's reign. In this way, we call those we serve from the idols of today to the living and true God and to the works "which God prepared beforehand, that we should walk in them."[24]

Liberation and the Cross

When the conspiratorial Pharisees prod Jesus to leave the area because Herod is out to kill him, he responds, "Go and tell that fox for me, 'Listen, I am casting out demons and performing cures today and tomorrow, and on the third day I finish my work.'" With these words, Jesus is not implying that he or his followers should be unconcerned with the decisions and policies of leaders and government. Rather, he is making it clear that they were not to have their actions determined by fear of others' decisions, but by the will and call of God. As followers of Jesus, our relationship to others is not to be reactionary, but Spirit-led. We are called not to a defensive posture, which expends time and effort to secure our position and privilege. A Christianity of privilege that seeks to stake out a special place for itself, that fights for laws that will secure its position, that acts as if it could craft a "Christian" nation legislatively, is not the Christianity of Jesus who took up his cross to rescue and deliver us. It is, rather an oppressive Christianity, for it walks over the sensibilities and visions of other voices, religious and non-religious. The Christianity of Jesus suffers and dies in order to serve. It loses itself for Christ and the gospel, for the sake of the world.

This way of operating includes the loss of worldly position and taking a stand "against the rulers, against the authorities, against the cosmic powers of this present darkness, against the spiritual forces of evil."[25] But this stance is always to be determined by our allegiance to the reign and will of God for the sake of serving. Our fight is against idolatrous power, not for the idolatry of ourselves as Christians and churches. Perpetua, an African young woman martyred in Carthage at the beginning of the third century, simply refused to recognize the Roman emperor as Lord and God. Her written testimony in prison gives witness to her faith and that of her companions and the deacons who came and served them in prison. Their simple refusal, along with many other Christians, to engage in the idolatry of the state, was a witness unto death. They were not trying to secure

24. Eph 2:10.
25. Eph 6:12.

themselves and their religion, but be witnesses to the sovereignty and ways of God.

This remains the calling of the followers of Jesus. What if we simply were known as those who stood against and resisted the idolatrous nationalism of our own time that raises our national security (with our expertise in killing) above all others, as well as the idolatries of race, class, power, and money? What if our society witnessed our fight against unjust, inequitable funding of public education, unrepresentative government, discriminatory hiring and housing practices, discrimination in the availability of health services, an unjust criminal justice system, biased sentencing of convicted persons, corporate environmental pollution, corporate greed, and unjust and corrupt ecclesiastical structures? What if it witnessed our push for concrete changes, including restoration and reparations? We would be giving witness to God's justice and ways of governing, and we would be taking up our cross, bearing the reaction of idolatrous powers. We would be a liberating church instead of a self-securing church.

This is not to say that we would be unconcerned for individuals and the effects of personal sin upon their daily lives and relationships, but our concern would not be like that of Pharisees circling their victim with stones in their hands. It would not be one of blanket judgments on groups of people. It would be the concern of sinners who experience God's grace reaching out from that experience to other sinners. It would be a concern for each individual's spiritual journey, with sensitivity to the context of their lives and the present ministry of the Spirit. It would be holistic. In entering into their hurts and suffering, we would take up our cross. And in these ways, we would also be a liberating church.

We see a white privileged form of Christianity in these United States of America. White privilege and a private Christianity are joined in an unholy alliance, in which many cultural "traditional values" are mixed in with a form of Christianity, and many middle-class values are sublimated behind a Christian mask. What Albert Pero wrote in 1988 concerning the "suburban captivity of the white church" remains relevant today. With this phrase, Pero suggests a church that seeks to isolate itself from the world's troubles, valuing its own security, property and possessions, comfort and convenience, above engagement with society's struggles. He believes that black churches (especially within predominantly white denominations) can have a "critical and reformatory" affect on white churches (at least those black churches that have not been "whitenized," but who are rooted in the church that, in slave days, while still enslaved, could sing, "Before I'll be a slave I'll be buried in my grave and go home to my Lord and be free.")[26] In white "suburbanized" churches, personal crisis is often that which opens individuals to the power of the gospel: the death of a child, the breakup of a marriage, addiction and the twelve-steps practice. Life itself often speaks a word to us, and we may begin steps outward. But the problem is that our white middle-class church may not be able to support additional steps into an ever-widening freedom to serve, to hear the cries, to enter into the suffering of others, and to be change agents at a societal level. We may find that we do not even have a theology that supports us. In the theology we receive, grace may mean God's acceptance, but not necessarily our transformation.

The liberating word of the cross must be proclaimed and lived. Therefore, we have much dying to do! The ministry of liberation to which we are called is dependent on God's power and faithfulness; therefore, we participate in the faithfulness of Jesus to God's liberating work. "God's righteousness comes through the faithfulness of Jesus Christ for all who have faith in him."[27] The dying we must undergo includes dying to trusting in our own power and resources, in and of ourselves (what Paul calls the flesh), and to those extensions of ourselves found in images to which we bow down. Among the idols of middle-class churches is the idol of comfort: "Don't take me out of my comfort zone and do not inconvenience me." We build walls around our comfort zones—these walls ensure that we remain in denial of our condition and lethargic about responding to God's call. Our lusts, possessiveness, consumerism, racism, and nationalism remain behind walls—hidden and unaddressed.

When Paul writes of our dying, it is to the power of this condition—to sin as a condition. "The death he died, he died to sin, once for all; but the life he lives, he lives to God. So you also must consider yourselves dead to sin and alive to God in Christ Jesus."[28] We die with Christ to this idolatrous condition daily, so that we might rise daily alive to God and to God's call. There is new life for us by God's grace. "Present your members to God as instruments of righteousness. For sin will have no dominion over you, since you are not under law but under grace."[29] We can come clean about our lives. Under God's mercy, we can come out of denial and darkness into

26. Pero and Moyo, *Theology and the Black Experience*, 227–48.

27. Rom 3:22 (CEB).

28. Rom 6:10–11.

29. Rom 6:13–14.

the light. There is dying to the false self and rising up into our true selves made in the image of God.

However, this always happens in concrete, specific ways through a process—a spiritual journey. When we change, it is always about that which is concrete and specific, never something general and abstract. The general confession of sins with which many churches begin worship is a helpful acknowledgment of what we need to be doing: to get specific. "I am an addict and my drug of choice is . . . " When we experience God's liberation, it is always from a particular bondage that Word and Spirit are bringing to our conscious awareness. Our agreement with the Spirit has us confronting a false attachment that holds us captive. Our "decision to turn our will and our lives" over to God is our being released by the power of the Spirit.

To use again the example of racism and white churches: if the circles of liberation are going to widen for white Christians, so that we move outward in the ministry of liberation in an increasingly diverse society, then we have to begin to be liberated concretely from our racism. We have to come out of our comfort zones, be willing to let our defenses come down (God will bring them down), become self-aware, listen to the impact of our attitudes upon others, and begin to acknowledge our bondage to racially inturned feelings and perceptions. Then, acknowledging our powerlessness over this addiction, we turn to God and God's power, which is the power of dying and rising, and allow God to release us outward. This process must become a way of life, a spiritual pattern in every aspect of our lives. Change takes time, and we must be patient with one another, just as God is patient. But above all, pastors and leaders who declare the word of repentance must expect such change because of God's victory in Christ and the power of the Spirit. The people we serve must come to have this anticipation of change and growth in ever-widening experiences of liberation to serve.

This journey begins with the word. ("So faith comes from what is heard, and what is heard comes through the word of Christ."[30]) Casting a vision of God's ways and governance and God's call upon our lives in Christ Jesus, we must call out that which has us bound and keeps us from the vision. We do this with confidence in the power of God to unbind. Our message is not one of laying a weight of guilt upon God's people, but a work of deliverance. Therefore, we speak the truth in love, with compassion for people who, like ourselves, are broken, forgiven, and welcomed by God into this liberating change.

30. Rom 10:17.

This journey of the cross and of dying continues, as we move outward into the suffering of others. As we experience our own brokenness and God's welcome and healing, we are freed to see the hurt of others without casting judgment. With the same graciousness that we experience, we communicate the liberating work of God in ever-widening dimensions, as that work encompasses the whole of human reality. When Paul writes that he has "become all things to all people, that [he] might by all means [liberate] some," he is expressing his own freedom to serve within the wide circle of humanity, the walls of hostility having come down.[31]

This journey, of course, is not only individual, but communal. It encompasses a community, as individuals who are on this journey find and experience each other, joining together in fellowship. Those responding to the call to turn from addictions and idols, to trust themselves to God's reign, gather with others who have entered this same door of deliverance. Together they are taken up in the work of God's reign, the work of setting captives free. They grow in the forms and ever-widening circles of liberation.

31. 1 Cor 9:22.

5

Community

We all meet at the foot of the cross. We meet before our Liberator at the point of our weakness and need. In the presence of our liberator God, who has come to us in Jesus, we are released into community, the dividing walls, the walls of hostility, egotism, possessiveness, and dominance having come down through God's Anointed. It is in our shared vulnerability and the experience of God's gracious liberating work that we truly find each other.

In the early years at St. Thomas, I made various attempts to gather members for Bible study in the middle of the week. There was a brief period when a group of the "very religious" met. Their tendency was to apply the words of the text to what was wrong with the world. It was deadly for anyone who, needy and broken, might venture in. It was only later in gatherings of sinners who confessed their sins to one another in openness to God's healing that community truly formed ("confess your sins to one another, and pray for one another, so that you may be healed"[1]).

It was our acknowledgment of need and our openness to God's liberation that opened us to others and began to give form to an open community. Others could come into our fellowship on a Sunday morning or at a midweek gathering and hear the community at prayer, crying out for God's help and thanking God for God's rescue, and feel that this was a place they could bring their problems. Among other messed-up people, they could bring their mess.

Needy people who acknowledge their own need welcome needy people. Those who do not acknowledge their need are affronted and even

1. Jas 5:16.

repulsed by those who do, by those who bring the reality too close to home. The truth is, "All have sinned and fall short of the glory of God."[2] When we do not acknowledge our need and brokenness, we judge others. As Paul writes, "In passing judgment on another you condemn yourself, because you, the judge, are doing the very same things."[3]

At some point in our lives, we must come to realize that our need is for God and for a fundamental "letting go." The journey we enter into is one of letting go, depending on God for power to do so. On this journey, we confess our relapses, keep turning to trust in God, and move on with sobriety. When drug addicts came to me with their ideas for reform, or how they wanted to make changes in their lives and relationships, I would say, "First things first." Until the addiction is addressed, nothing else matters. It is like rearranging the chairs on the Titanic as it sinks. You are still going down, and will continue to make a mess of life and relationships. (This is why pastors and leaders must address addictions and idolatries, rather than simply talk about how Christians ought to live. The central issue is spiritual, not moral.)

But when we realize our helplessness, receive God's help, and join with others who need God, we see ourselves in them, and the barriers to loving service come down. The distance between us and others narrows, and we become a welcoming community less inclined to secure ourselves from the other.

We hired a recovering addict to be our janitor. He testified that he had been a predator (as a gang member) and now, by the grace of God, was a responsible citizen. After being with us for some months, he shared his gratitude with us: "You were the first people to give me the keys to your building. Being trusted has deeply affected me." He went on to receive an advanced degree in counseling, and now counsels addicts at a neighborhood hospital. His experience reveals both the central nature of spiritual transformation and the place of the community of grace in that process. He was being trusted by the community because love saw who he was becoming through God's liberating work, and because love's work is not centered in securing ourselves or our buildings.

People experiencing God's deliverance generally find themselves reaching out to others in need. They seek out lost, hurting, needy people. Rochelle, a recovering addict, reached out to women in a nearby recovery

2. Rom 3:23.
3. Rom 2:1.

house and brought Liz into our fellowship. After being with us for about a year, Liz felt it was time to leave the recovery house and suggested moving into the parish house that was adjacent to the church. It was being used for offices and meetings, but there was room. I brought her request to the church council: Liz, who had spent three years in jail, one year in the recovery house, and had little more than a year of clean time, wanted to move into the parish house. The council prayed about it and said they believed the "Lord was in it." There was a time when our church council would not have even considered such a request. But we had been undergoing a spiritual liberation and transformation. This sister in Christ was not so distant from those on the present council. We all had come to face addictions and idolatries in our lives (not necessarily drug addictions, but addictions nevertheless). We had come to know God's grace and the leading of the Spirit. We were being set free to trust God, and the security of our property was not among our highest priorities. Within a few months, we gave Liz the keys to the church building; she was empowered to be a steward of the property. Above all, she became an intercessor for the church.

The community of addicts (drug and non-drug) liberated by grace are sent out to those in need to bring them into the fold of God's grace. They are invited to stand at the foot of the cross with us. Those who are in need of liberation are, of course, all around us, in our families and neighborhoods.

I preached at a revival service in Montana under a large white tent along the side of a highway. There were a number of Lutheran churches involved in this ministry. In the sermon, I illustrated a point with reference to a recovering drug addict. After the sermon, a woman said to me that they did not meet many addicts in their area of rural Montana. She was sharing from her experience and that of others with whom she spent time. But her view that there were not many addicts in her part of the world was not accurate to the situation. Pastors of these churches, sharing with my revival partner and myself, relayed the serious problem with addictions they encountered in their ministries, especially methamphetamine addiction. And, prior to the sermon, a woman gave a testimony of being freed from alcoholism by the grace of God. So, it was not that there was little addiction in the area, but that the circles this woman traveled in kept her from the problem. Or, to put it another way, the buffer of affluence, the commitment to one's own comfort zone and to people she was comfortable with, kept her from seeking those lost to drug addiction. For her to be involved in a Jesus kind of ministry, which involves seeking and rescuing the lost, she would have to be liberated from her own addictions—especially those of comfort and convenience.

Early in my ministry at St. Thomas, it became clear to me that drug addiction was a problem among some of the young adults. But it had been hidden away by their families. I engaged two members, one a young adult and the other a recovering alcoholic, in a series of classes on ministering to addicts. These classes were offered at a faith-based hospital. Soon after, we invited Narcotics Anonymous to hold meetings at our church. This was the beginning of a ministry to addicts, which took on a life of its own as recovering addicts took leadership for the ministry. The point is this: we *chose* this ministry; we chose to reach out to addicts. It was not that drug addiction was a greater problem in our urban setting or among communities of color (a stereotype fed by the media). For years, health statistics have shown that it has been a larger problem among whites. One of the primary reasons for the stereotype is that the "drug war" has largely been fought in urban communities of color rather than in white suburbs or frat houses on college campuses.[4] We had a ministry to addicts at St. Thomas because we *chose* to reach out to addicts with the good news of liberation.

Jesus made clear that his ministry was to the poor and needy. When John the Baptist was in prison and having doubts about whether Jesus was "the one who is to come," he sent followers to question Jesus. Jesus said to them, "Go back and report to John what you have seen and heard: The blind receive sight, the lame walk, those who have leprosy are cleansed, the deaf hear, the dead are raised, and the good news is proclaimed to the poor."[5] Jesus also said, "When you give a luncheon or dinner, do not invite your friends, your brothers or sisters, your relatives, or your rich neighbors; if you do, they may invite you back and so you will be repaid. But when you give a banquet, invite the poor, the crippled, the lame, the blind, and you will be blessed."[6] In other words, do not stay in your comfort zone, but reach out to those who are hurting. This is a basic expectation Jesus has of his followers: "The poor you will always have with you, and you can help them any time you want."[7]

"The poor you will always have with you." They may be hidden from you, from your comfort zone, from the circles in which you operate. But

---

4. For great clarity on this issue, see Alexander, *The New Jim Crow.*

5. Luke 7:22.

6. Luke 14:13.

7. Mark 14:7.

they are there. The federal government's poverty line (for a family of four) is an income of $24,000 per year. The counties in America that have the least number of poor generally have around 10 percent, and most counties have far more. In many counties, a quarter or even a third of the population is poor. There is a slightly higher poverty rate outside urban centers than within.[8] The issue is not where are "the poor, the crippled, the lame, the blind," but where is the church?

I hope it is becoming clear that "consciousness raising" alone is not the answer. We need recovery and liberation from addictions to comfort, possessions, money, pleasure, power, status, class, race, and so many other obsessions. On the one hand, we must gain clarity concerning the radical call of God and the new life and alternate lifestyle into which Jesus leads us. On the other hand, we must experience the actual need for God to heal us and deliver us into this new life. We need the kind of spiritual crisis all addicts go through, where life hangs in the balance and we are faced with *deciding* "to turn our will and our lives over to the care of God." Then we may find ourselves crying out, "God have mercy on me." Churches are liberated as individual members are liberated.

As members experience liberation, they begin to be models to others of what a liberated and liberating church looks like. At St. Thomas, it was especially recovering addicts that first modeled the liberated community. Rochelle, mentioned above, came into our fellowship reaching out for help. Her children had come to our summer program, so there already had been a relationship to the church. She reached out for help with her addiction. She received prayer and counsel from myself and the recovering alcoholic who had been part of our addiction recovery ministry training. She came to Sunday worship and prayed during community prayer time. We would gather in a circle for prayer and members would thank God for their family, for their health, for their church, and she would call out to God with a loud voice to have mercy on her, to deliver her from her bondage. With tears, runny nose, a body doubling over and loud cries, she made a scene. Some members told her she should pray like that at home, not in the dignified atmosphere of our sanctuary. But God answered her and delivered her. As God was restoring her to sanity and her clean time was growing, she started praying for other issues in her life, such as her relationship with her husband and her children, sharing her brokenness with us as she opened herself to God. She also gave praise to God and expressed deep gratitude

8. www.povertyusa.org.

for the healing work God was doing in her life. Her witness to God's actual, concrete, liberating activity gave hope to others, and her prayers gave permission to others to also call out to God. Others, addicted, abused, anxious about their children and relationships and finances, called out to God with specifics. We began to get a model of the church at the foot of the cross, the church God calls forth, the church of God's liberating transforming activity.

Liberated people become liberating people. Recovering drug addicts reach out to other addicts. Rochelle reached out to the recovery house, brought clothes and other items to the women, and prayed with them. She joined with two other recovering addicts in what we came to call the Seventy-Ninth Street Ministry, sharing with others in the streets the good news of God's liberation.

Needy people of all kinds, discovering God's generosity and good gifts, reach out to needy people. This is true for those who come to realize that they have an addiction to comfort or pleasure or money that distances them from God and loving action toward others, and then cry out to God for deliverance. It is true of those who discover, as Paul did, that they are in bondage to a self-made righteousness that has them persecuting others with demeaning judgments, and then reach out to God for help. God rescues them, and they begin to experience themselves and others differently. They have liberating news to share that others need to know, and with which they must reach out.

People being liberated make a different set of decisions than people still active in their addiction. They will no longer "use" with those with whom they shared an addiction. But they will encourage them into a twelve-step program or to their church, if their church is about deliverance and recovery. They may be involved in an intervention in which family members and friends gather around the addicted person, to share the impact of their addiction upon their lives, with the goal of getting them into treatment. The intervention is intended to help bring forward the crisis that must happen—the decision that must be made—and the crying out for God's help that opens freedom's door. Expect this pattern, no matter what the addiction is.

Expect this pattern when it comes to the middle-class-values captivity of the church. People being freed from addiction to values of comfort, convenience, pleasure, money, possessions, and self-satisfaction, make a different set of decisions. They have a desire to spend time in the presence of the God who is freeing them; worship and prayer become important.

Their lives become simpler. They want to know God's will for themselves: "What do you want me to do with my life, God, since it is yours (since it no longer belongs to all these other things)"? They see the needs of others and are willing to go where the needs are, with the gifts for serving that God gives. They begin to make a different set of decisions.

Congregations come to make a different set of decisions as individual members are being liberated. There was a time when I dreaded church council meetings, either because of the conflict I expected or because of the long discussions over issues far removed from our purpose. That changed as we changed (as individuals changed), so that meetings increasingly became a time to strategize for the outward movement of God's liberating work.

When using the liturgy for "Holy Communion in Special Circumstances" with the home-bound or hospitalized, I loved to say the words, "In great love you sent to us Jesus, your Son, who reached out to heal the sick and suffering, who preached good news to the poor, and who, on the cross, opened his arms to all." This reaching out that Jesus did is the same reaching out he gives his followers to do. This is what the body of Christ looks like when it is being Christ's concrete expression in the world. "Reaching out" means we go to where the sick, suffering, and poor are and, like Jesus, spend time there, enter into the struggles, and with them open ourselves to God's healing work.

When on vacation, I went to a large suburban church, the parking lot filled with recent-model cars. When I came out of the church and headed for my car, I was stopped by a man who needed emergency help. He had talked to members of the church and was told that he would have to come back on Tuesday and meet with the committee that did that sort of thing. This church had an emphasis on global mission, but was not prepared to respond to basic local needs. Reaching out and engaging others means being willing to be inconvenienced. Convenience is one of the first idols some have to face, when, in obedience to Jesus' call, they reach out.

Needy people need the body of Christ. They need the community. I recall being at a revival service at a neighboring church, where a number of young men gave their testimonies. Over and over again, one young man after another, in referring to their liberation, used the phrase "by the grace of God *and* All Peoples Church." People experience God's grace in and through community and the various gifts and ministries of Christ's body. In the end, not only individuals must be liberated to reach out to "heal the sick and suffering and proclaim good news to the poor," but the church as a whole. Pastors and leaders must start (along with themselves) with those who are "getting it"—for they will begin to model the church that God is raising up.

The simple act of reaching out engages us in ever-widening circles of liberation as congregations. Our common vision and sense of mission comes from the kind of engagement that obedience to Christ calls forth. Some kinds of liberating work we do not see ourselves doing until we take steps in response to Christ's call. So much of our vision is determined by unacknowledged addictions, prejudices, and fears that, until we start following Jesus and keep taking steps, we will see little of our true mission as God's people. Congregations—especially those in bondage to middle-class values—have to be on a journey of decisively reaching out to the poor and suffering. This is a way for them to increasingly face and be freed from those false attachments they have denied. The act of following Jesus where he leads will have us truly dealing with our condition. Spiritual liberation and concretely embodying that liberation in action are integral to our growth in serving.

Jesus took three disciples up a mountain, where they experienced the light of God in the face of Christ. They received an awe-filled revelation of God's action in Christ. When they came down from the mountain (we always must come down!), they immediately were involved in and training for ministry. They were met by a man whose son was afflicted by a spirit. "It convulses him until he foams at the mouth; it mauls him and will scarcely leave him."[9] This man had already come to Jesus' disciples—those who had remained at the bottom of the mountain, disciples who had been trained by Jesus. [10] Although they had previously exercised the authority Jesus gave them, here they were helpless before the plight of this oppressed boy. And Jesus was not happy about their failure to believe. "Jesus answered, 'You faithless and perverse generation, how much longer must I be with you and bear with you?'"[11]

In Matthew's version of this story, the disciples ask Jesus privately, "'Why could we not cast it out?' He said to them, 'Because of your little

9. Luke 9:39.

10. Earlier in this ninth chapter of Luke, Jesus is depicted sending out the twelve and giving them "power and authority over all demons and to cure diseases, and . . . to proclaim the kingdom of God and to heal." And we read that "they . . . went through the villages, bringing the good news and curing diseases everywhere."

11. Luke 9:41.

faith. For truly I tell you, if you have faith the size of a mustard seed, you will say to this mountain, 'Move from here to there,' and it will move; and nothing will be impossible for you.'"[12] In Mark, Jesus' answer is "This kind can come out only through prayer." We are reminded that faith (Matthew) and prayer (Mark) are integrally related and that we are radically dependent on God for the ministry of liberation to which God calls us. But the other thing we notice that is critical for this discussion, is that these disciples tried! They attempted to minister deliverance to this boy, in response to the pleas of this father. In the process, they were faced with their unbelief—but also open for further instruction and empowerment.

Certainly, this must also be the movement of individuals and congregations. Attempts must be made, failures experienced, and our faithlessness exposed, so that growth and outward action of God's liberating work can continue. First steps have to be taken and first struggles endured, preparing the way for later steps and struggles. The steps taken always involve sacrifice and a change in priorities. This can take the form of releasing funds to support organizations on the front lines of addressing domestic and global hunger, or hands-on involvement through church programs (food pantry, tutoring, literacy program, job training, providing work for those who have received alternate sentencing to community service or those released from prison, working with at-risk children and their families). In ministry to those who are sick, hurting, and grieving, a cross is taken up. And this ministry is always a sharing the good news of God's reign of justice, mercy, and faithfulness. As individuals are being released outward (freed from idols), their vision and gifts connect with the needs of the community in a "natural" movement (in contrast to a forced program).

For congregations in captivity to middle-class values, the most distant circle in this outward movement is generally that of addressing systemic oppression, because it involves politics (and our comfortable ideologies are slow to break up). I recall listening to a testimony years ago—it was on a cassette tape—of a very wealthy white woman. She had been born to wealth and lived in a mansion in New York, but she was brought low by alcoholism. Her addiction had crushed her personally, destroyed relationships, and left her alone and in despair. It was at that point that she experienced being found by God. The Good Shepherd brought her home and liberated her into a new life. At some point in her spiritual journey, she decided to give up her wealth and live like "ordinary" people. She moved to Arizona

12. Matt 17:19–20.

(as I recall) and had a house built in an ordinary middle-class neighborhood. But when she came to move in, she realized that she had built the biggest house among her neighbors. When we are released from an addiction and begin the journey outward, we have little sense of the distance we must travel and the changes we will undergo. By the grace of God, we face those changes as we continue to face addictions. And by God's grace, we are sustained in opening ourselves to new freedoms and the demolishing of old ideologies that never reflected reality.

"The poor you will always have with you." They are not far away. It is inconvenience and discomfort that distances the affluent from the poor. It can be inconvenient and uncomfortable to see the poor as "one of us" and to face our prejudices and preconceptions about poverty—about who is poor and why. The spanning of the distance is a spiritual journey of letting "the same mind be in [us] that was in Christ Jesus, who, though he was in the form of God, did not regard equality with God as something to be exploited, but emptied himself, taking the form of a slave, being born in human likeness. And being found in human form, he humbled himself and became obedient to the point of death—even death on a cross."[13]

Stay the journey and "the other" becomes us. "We are all beggars." We are all needy. None of us can stand on our own merit for what we have. Everything is a gift. If we have found bread, we share with a beggar who has none. This is certainly the reality, but we have to confront the lie we have believed.

Some of us, in this nation, have been "privileged" by a white supremacist history, but operate oblivious to it. We act as though we have "pulled ourselves up by our own bootstraps," ignoring the degree to which we have "advanced" by riding on the backs of others. America has been crafted by racism to work for us. Unlike others among us, our cultures were not torn down by slavery and racism. Rather, doors were engineered to open for us. I was dropping off an African-American member of my congregation. He was just getting out of the car when police came up behind us with lights flashing and pulled around in front of us, blocking my car. Two white police officers got out of their car, and my brother in Christ immediately raised his hands in the air (I never raise my hands in the air with police—unless they tell me to do so) and informs them that he was just coming from a Bible Study, and the driver was his pastor. One of the police officers who had arrived at my car window then asked about my profession. I told him

13. Phil 2:5–8.

I was a pastor. The police immediately got back into their car and drove off without any explanation as to why we were stopped. I was not accustomed to receiving no explanation from the police. My African-American brother was. I do not want racism to give me privilege, but it does. It is systemic and pervasive. So, I must work and pray for change in society, in individuals, and myself.

As I begin to face the addiction to and the intractable nature of racism, systemic and personal, I experience my powerlessness, which is not a bad beginning. Step One: "We admit we are powerless over what we are attached to and dependent on, and our lives—left to ourselves—are unmanageable."

This helplessness is true as well for seeing ourselves in the other, when the experience of the other is so different from our own (when my experience of the police is so different from that of my African-American friend). We make a start when we acknowledge our distance from others and our helplessness to bridge the distance. The beginning of our liberation is confession. The next step is to turn our lives over to the care of God. This step of trust is, at the same time, a step toward openness to others. Openness makes possible the receiving into ourselves, to whatever extent our imagination makes possible, a sense and feel for what others are enduring. It begins to give us ears to hear, so that we do not immediately dismiss what we are hearing based on our limited experience or our ideologies. There has been much talk in recent decades about multicultural congregations. But it has been very difficult to move beyond the talk. The path is clearly narrow and the journey hard. This is especially true when it comes to communities formed of black and white Americans, given the history and legacy of racism. It seems to me that the straightest line for the forming of such communities is for white people to join black churches, to be open and be changed.

We need the others' experience. We need the radical fellowship of Jesus where the dividing walls come down. But those of us who have grown up white in America carry so much baggage that gets in the way of receiving from others. We need to place ourselves in a position where we will be challenged to lay down this baggage that burdens us. The formation of multicultural communities is not simply a matter of including a diversity of music styles in worship and tweaking the liturgy. The congregation must be on a journey of spiritual and embodied liberation, personal, social, and political. The way of liberation must be proclaimed and lived. Personal transformation and social justice, relationships within the body of Christ and the reaching out and welcoming others without partiality, these must be emphasized, expected, and grown into. Everyone who comes into the congregation must breathe in a liberating atmosphere, feel the impact of the liberating Spirit and Word, and realize that here everyone can unburden themselves. Here there is mercy. Here there is deliverance. Here we meet at the foot of the cross. Here our gifts are received.

"Gracious God, raise up such a community." If we have a sense of what is truly needed, we know that this is a work that only God can do. Yes, through us—but not without surrender and prayer. We are, like the boy with a "mute and deaf spirit," held captive to false attachments and unable to speak or hear the word. And, as it was for the disciples who could not deliver the boy from the unclean spirit, so also it is with us. We need to hear Jesus' word again: "This kind can come out only through prayer." This sort of change takes Holy Spirit power!

Diversity

My denomination has traditionally emphasized the priesthood of all believers and the vocation of Christians in the world. We are all gifted and called. Within the congregation, which is a training ground for serving in the world, there can be a great diversity of ministries. But the middle-class-values captivity of the church has often limited the expression of that reality. Little is expected beyond support roles for assisting with worship ritual: assisting ministers, acolytes, readers, altar servers, choir singers, Sunday School teachers, members of the council, or property caretakers. In congregations experiencing renewal and the liberating work of the Spirit, however, there are other forms of service increasingly being manifested: members (other than the pastor) involved in prayer ministry, spiritual counseling, providing guidance into the way of liberation, visiting the sick, prison ministry, preaching, prophetic words and actions, showing mercy, welcoming others with the welcome of Christ, social justice action, organizing for action, leading Bible Studies, spiritually perceptive teaching, and many others. We have seen this widening of lay ministry in pentecostal and charismatic movements. Although, in many white charismatic churches, ministry tends to be personalized to the point of virtually eliminating any social justice emphasis.

The Spirit widens both our forms of ministry and our circles of ministry. We are being released and equipped for ministry to people struggling, hurting, being pressed down and pushed to the edge. We are not interested in recruiting members or having people switch churches. It is about going out to the highways and byways. We are not concerned about our denominational "brand." Denominationalism is over. Increasingly, the people we reach out to are not interested in denominations, but in what is *real*. At St. Thomas, we made little of being Lutheran—but made much of being the body of Christ. We acknowledged our denomination and recognized the importance of being a part of a wider body of Christians for accountability and joint action. We celebrated the reality of grace and the gospel central to Lutheran theology. But we did not act like we were the only ones who knew grace was central. We saw ourselves as ecumenical. Some became active in our life and mission, but never became members; they felt unable (as they saw it) to cut ties with the tradition in which they were raised and move to another. Generally, those coming from little or no church background simply found a life-giving, healing community. Richard Foster, in his book *Streams of Living Water: Celebrating the Great Traditions of Christian Faith*, considers various traditions as streams flowing from Christ, the Living Water.[14] At St. Thomas, we felt, in one way or another, the various streams: the contemplative, holiness, charismatic, social justice, evangelical, and incarnational.

As the Spirit widens the shape and circles of ministry, the makeup of a congregation changes—its demographics become diverse. Internally, we now must increasingly face the societal barriers that previously had been largely external to our congregation's life and implicitly chosen mission. The walls that come down by God's grace have entered the sanctuary. We get to experience more deeply the reality of that grace.

That is what happened for the church in Corinth. The assembly of God in Corinth was made up of Jews and Gentiles, rich and poor. These young Christians were "not lacking in any spiritual gift"; however, they were spiritually immature, operating by their own strength, resources, desires, and attitudes, rather than the guidance of the Spirit. Their giftedness was based in God's gracious giving; their maturity awaited their growth. At that point, the decisions they made and steps taken in regard to divisions over personalities, gifts, and class would make for their spiritual growth. Paul pointed them in the direction away from "the flesh" towards the ways of Christ and the Spirit.

---

14. Foster, *Streams of Living Water*.

When it came to class, Paul observed that "not many of you were wise by human standards, not many were powerful, not many were of noble birth"—which is to say, some of you were of noble birth and powerful (by human standards). But as was true of Roman society, not many were noble or powerful; most were poor and illiterate. Here in this assembly was a cross section of Corinthian society, which is what we would expect if the gospel of liberation is for all and goes out to all. We would also expect that it came at the point of people's need, rich or poor. The next words of Paul emphasize this:

> But God chose what is foolish in the world to shame the wise; God chose what is weak in the world to shame the strong; God chose what is low and despised in the world, things that are not, to reduce to nothing things that are, so that no one might boast in the presence of God. He is the source of your life in Christ Jesus, who became for us wisdom from God, and righteousness and sanctification and redemption, in order that, as it is written, "Let the one who boasts, boast in the Lord."[15]

They had all come into the assembly of God by responding to the message of God's liberation through Christ Jesus. Together they celebrated new life in Christ. They were energized by the pouring out of the Spirit and the gifts that were given without partiality. They were amazed that the Spirit allotted "to each one individually just as the Spirit chooses," rather than according to one's standing in Roman society. Even slaves could be leaders in the assembly, as the Spirit chose. (Urbanus, who is greeted as a "co-worker in Christ" in Romans 16, has a common slave name. Also of note, among those greeted in Romans is a woman named Junia who is "prominent among the apostles.") And yet, the class structure remained and existed among the assembled believers in Corinth. The liberating work of God was gathering people from the various strata of Roman society, who, having been brought from their separate places, now had the opportunity to live out the reality of walls coming down "in Christ." Their very existence together as sisters and brothers in Christ demanded that they face the false power structure they had assumed, and upon which they had depended out in the world.

Therefore, Paul was bound to call them, as a community, deeper into the Christ reality, as class divisions could be seen when they gathered for the love feast, the Lord's supper. Those who were wealthy came early; slaves, who had to finish their work, came later. And the first to arrive started

15. 1 Cor 1:27–31.

eating before the others came; some even got drunk! Paul wrote of their contempt for the assembly of God: they "humiliate those who have nothing." The way forward was to discern the body; they were all individually members of the same body—Christ's body. The new, liberating work God was doing would release them from the oppressive divisions and attitudes in the world. The steps they must take were clear and practical: examine themselves, recognize their unity in Christ, and "when you come together to eat, wait for one another."

In the community of liberation, we learn to leave past values and priorities behind. As we reach out to others in need with the gospel, God gathers a diverse community, for God comes for all. That diversity becomes the training ground for our next liberating steps. We enter into the lives of others whose experiences are not the same as ours, whose struggles are not simply like ours. The love of God poured into our hearts by the Spirit requires us to listen and gain insight. Preconceptions about "the other" have to die and be replaced by compassionate understanding. Our vision enlarges, the circle for God's liberating work widens—we can no longer ignore systemic oppression.

The very commitment and act, on the part of the affluent, of reaching out to walk with those who are poor, exposes our addiction to comfort and convenience. It also begins to reveal the nature and causes of poverty. Our ideologies have made simple what is complex. Reality faces us with disturbing questions about ourselves and our society. Where is the justice in the children of the affluent receiving greater resources and educational programs than the poor? Where is the justice in children going to school hungry and unable to concentrate on their studies? Where is the justice in taking fathers or mothers out of their homes and imprisoning them for drug-related offenses, when the need is for treatment? Where is the justice in not responding to the emotional and psychological needs of children, however those needs came to be? Where is the justice in ignoring the impact of race and class on these realities and on the decisions made by legislators? At a most basic level, we have to acknowledge with Augustine, "The superfluities of the rich are the necessities of the poor."[16]

Congregations that engage themselves in the lives of others (other "others"—those different from us), welcoming, listening, including, receiving help for their mission to all, are deepened in God's liberating work, being changed from one degree of liberation to another. They may end

16. From Augustine's commentary on Psalm 147:12; see Kelly, *Saint Augustine*, 183.

up being smaller congregations, but with widening ministry. In the sixties, there was a church growth movement that emphasized homogeneity among congregants as a way to numerically grow congregations. Where practiced, it seemed to work, but at the expense of deepening spiritual growth and commitment. Many such churches have become large worship centers, divorced from the plight of others in need and suffering oppression. Instead of being salt, light, and yeast in the world, they gather once a week to sit down for a spiritual feast among themselves.

A Light to the Nation

Frederick Douglass wrote of the "sham religion which everywhere prevailed." By this, he meant the slaveholders who would beat slaves every day but the Sabbath, savagely oppressing fellow human beings, but on the Sabbath would serve as deacons and leaders in churches. The slaveholder would maintain daily prayers and Bible reading, while ensuring that his slaves could not learn to read.[17] This was a form of Christianity captive to the slave system. It was a sham. Something similar could be said of a Christianity in which the American flag, whiteness, "traditional" cultural values, money, and political power are wrapped up in *our* Jesus and *our* personal salvation. Such an idolatrous Christianity is a sham that reveals itself often in merciless reaction to the other, the one on the outside of our privileged religion; it is devoid of discernment, as manifest in an "evangelical" president of a Christian college endorsing Donald Trump in glowing terms as living "a life of loving and helping others as Jesus taught." The sad reality is that this extraordinary blindness and sham religion is pervasive. In an increasingly non-religious society, the prevalence of this kind of so-called Christianity is often what others consider Christianity and the church to be. In the midst of this reality, God calls forth a people who will be light in the darkness—not only as individuals, but as communities.

Jesus was speaking to his community of followers when he said, "You are the light of the world . . . Let your light shine before others, so that they may see your good works and give glory to your Father in heaven."[18] It is not only as individuals that we are to do this, but as communities of liberation. As congregations, liberation must be our mission. We must proclaim it, organize for it and let go of whatever keeps us from it. This is the freedom

17. Douglass, *Life and Times*, 75.
18. Matt 5:14–16.

74

for which Christ has set us free. And it is the freedom we are to communicate and live. That communication and action demands discernment and recognizing the signs of the times.

6

Praxis

Pastors are often practical theologians within the context of the congregation's mission in the world. Yes, they are teachers of "the faith." But even more than this, they are called to be attentive to what faith demands in the moment (that is, where the Spirit is leading). They are not simply passing on a belief system, but, along with other leaders, equipping the saints for ministry within the community of faith and in the world. Therefore, pastors, along with other leaders, must be forward-looking. They ask, "What next"? They must not only attend to "theological truths," but acknowledge the situation of the people they serve and the world into which they are sent, heeding God's call in the present. For faith to act through love, it must have knowledge—practical knowledge—that comes from engagement with the world in an ever-widening context.

The subject matter of practical theology has been described as "everyone and everything."[1] It concerns being engaged in this world, in all its dimensions and with its various power structures, in order to bring about change. The work of practical theologians, as Joyce Ann Mercer sees it, "is present and future oriented rather than focusing primarily upon the past. Practical theologians work toward transformation—a recognition that practical theological work takes place not merely for the sake of inquiry per se, but in order to make a difference in people's lives and in the world."[2] It has a transcendental and prophetic element. Andrew Root calls for the recognition of transcendence. He points to the experience of God's presence

1. Rahner, *Theological Investigations, Volume 9*, 101–14.
2. Mercer, "Feminism and Womanist Practical Theology," 101.

in real, concrete human beings. He sees this lacking in much of practical theology, and yet it is concretely the experience of many.[3] And Karl Rahner points out that practical theology involves reflection "which sees into the future, seeking what is to be done here and now, extending the horizons of the possible future, trying the spirits which are proclaiming the future, then the process of reflection upon it, scientifically organized."[4] His reference to a discerning process that is prior to a scientific organization acknowledges that there is a practical knowing, the dynamic of which is different from a speculative theorizing. This practical knowing and theology that looks to the future—and therefore to what ought to be—is not simply an application of dogmatic or theoretical theology. It has its own dynamic.

I see pastors and leaders in the church as practical theologians, on the front lines. I had not been long in parish ministry before I was reading less theoretical theology and more psychology, sociology, political analysis, and history. I sought out writings on trauma, abuse, addiction, racism; liberationist thought, womanist interpretation, urban studies and writings by other pastors grappling with the same issues as I was encountering. I took up discussions with local pastors from diverse denominational backgrounds. In addition, as I increasingly had members and leaders in my congregation with a lively sense of mission and ministry, I was engaged with their insights and analysis of our situation and discernment for action. As I see it now, all of this was an element in doing practical theology, where real ministry meets real people. This theology and knowledge is accumulative. I think of Jesus' words, "Every scribe who has been trained for the kingdom of heaven is like the master of a household who brings out of his treasure what is new and what is old."[5]

In addition to this accumulated treasure, this historical and empirical element, there is a transcendental element. "For all who are led by the Spirit of God are children of God."[6] Mainline historic denominations like my own (Lutheran) have tended to pride themselves in their accumulated treasure, both old and new. Their strength can be seen in their openness and engagement with the modern world, with its *theoria* and *praxis*, while retaining their identity and roots. But they have been weak on the transcendental aspect, on the activity of the Spirit; fortunately, however, there are

---

3. Root, *Christopraxis*, 51.
4. Rahner, *Theological Investigations, Volume 9*, 103.
5. Matt 13:52.
6. Rom 8:14.

signs of change in renewal movements, retreats, spiritual exercises, spiritual direction, and so on. (There has to be change in order for the church to *be* the church.) Pastors and theologians at times have joked about the "forgotten person of the Trinity." If we have forgotten, then we must get intentional about remembering. It is telling that in the New Testament—brimming with practical action, real ministry to real human beings—the words "Spirit," "spirit," or "spirits" are used over three hundred fifty times. By comparison, *The Wiley Blackwell Companion to Practical Theology*, with fifty-six chapters (over six hundred pages) of essays on praxis, uses Spirit or spirit to refer to God, or humanity as related to God (in the body of the text), by my digital count, thirty-nine times.[7] Of course, experience with the Spirit can take many forms and be expressed without reference to the Spirit. The Spirit operates with a kind of anonymity; we even expect a degree of that anonymity when practical theology deals with contemporary issues of ministry, mission, and social justice. Nevertheless, a theology of praxis must also be a theology of the Spirit, and the use of the word "Spirit" is kin to our use of "God." We may have various philosophical constructs for God—being itself, the ground of being (Tillich), absolute esse, incomprehensible mystery (Rahner)—but we still incessantly come back to the word "God." At some point we must acknowledge, as Jesus did, that the "Spirit is upon us" to do something.

At the heart of Christian praxis is the power of the Spirit, as well as the particularity of Jesus and the universality of Christ. We are to place ourselves in the gospel narratives not only with the disciples of Jesus, but with Jesus himself. ("I have set you an example, that you also should do as I have done to you."[8]) Jesus is the example of our true humanity. Abiding "in Christ" makes the example inward, Christ formed in us. The Spirit bears witness with our spirit, not only to our being children of God, but to the timely action to which we are called. Practical action flows from the treasure store of those "trained for the kingdom of heaven" *and* by the power and leading of the Spirit. Both the treasure and the Spirit are necessary: Word and Spirit.

---

7. Miller-McLemore, *Wiley-Blackwell Companion*.

8. John 13:15.

Jesus as Example

In Jesus, we see our true humanity. We see it in his God-centeredness and submission to God's will. We see it in his other-oriented relationships that take the form of concrete action. We see it in the ways he operates, with compassion and in the power of God, to bring healing and deliverance. We see it, above all, in his gracious welcome of the outcast, the poor, the despised, the abused, and the broken.

Jesus' teaching is one with his other actions. It gives expression to a humanity that finds its true being in union with God and, therefore, with creation and our sister, brother creatures. The good news of the nearness of God's reign speaks to the reality of God as our center and that that reality is not far away. It is readily available to all who turn from false centers (anything that suggests itself as an alternative center) and turn to God. It is readily available because God graciously helps us with our turning.

Humanity, when it is an expression of being in God (in other words, being its true self), expresses itself in ways similar to Jesus. Its actions manifest tangible compassion in care for the poor and outcast, in love for the enemy, in commitment to transformation and healing. It has a "Jesus look" to it. That is why we experience a radical dissonance with a form of Christianity that ignores the poor, that lives in fear of people who are different, that is ready to build walls to keep the refugee out, that excludes, demeans, and dismisses.

The beatitudes give expression to our true humanity and to action.[9] As we come to find our life and center in God, we allow ourselves to mourn—there is much to mourn about—and we experience comfort, for God is our comforter. In God, we experience ourselves as lowly; from that vantage point, we know the earth is ours—for all is a gift from God. We hunger for justice and operate with hope, for we know there is justice with God. With the mercy we have experienced, we are enabled to be merciful, and we likewise experience more mercy, "a good measure, pressed down, shaken together and running over."[10] In God, we are coming to will one thing, in the place of double-mindedness, which gives us eyes to see and ears to hear. In God, who is our peace in the midst of the storm, we become instruments of peace. Since God is about peace, reconciliation, and unity, we are called children of God. In God, we find we must stand against injustice. We risk

9. Matt 5:1–12.
10. Luke 6:38.

being slapped down in our stand for the sake of justice, but this is the way it is with God's reign.

The blessing of being in God is in contrast with the "curse" of living away from God, as we have it in Luke:

> Woe to you who are rich, for you have already received your comfort. Woe to you who are well fed now, for you will go hungry. Woe to you who laugh now, for you will mourn and weep. Woe to you when everyone speaks well of you, for that is how their ancestors treated the false prophets.[11]

With these words, Jesus places before us the foundational nature of praxis. It is tied up with our being *in God*, without whom we lose our humanity. When we lose our humanity, we laugh when we ought to weep and live full while others live without. We worry over pleasing others, when we ought to stand up for justice and righteousness.

We cannot separate who we are from what we do. We can say, "I accept Christ, I accept Christ," using those easy words as a cover for a life that has no real connection to Jesus' lived life; our praxis will be disconnected from the words. "Not everyone who says to me, 'Lord, Lord,' will enter the kingdom of heaven, but only the one who does the will of my Father in heaven."[12] The point is this: If there is movement of our being into God, we will be undergoing change in the actions we take at the same time, for the one flows from the other. Our relationship to God matters for genuine and fundamental transformation.

The praxis and example of Jesus serves both as a mirror for examining our actions and for recognizing our true humanity. We can imagine ourselves in Jesus' place, noticing what he, our older brother, says about himself. We can see if it fits with our experience of our own humanity. We encounter Jesus in the witness of the first followers as they passed on what they received. We meet him as his life and teaching came to be applied in communities who bowed their hearts to the Crucified and Risen One and from which the gospel narratives were formed. With gratitude for this witness, we attempt to see ourselves, not only in the place of disciples, but in the form and practice of Jesus. Without taking anything away from the uniqueness of Jesus, we endeavor to see our humanity in his.

11. Luke 6:24–26.
12. Matt 7:21.

In the Gospel of John, Jesus says, "I am the light of the world. Whoever follows me will never walk in darkness but will have the light of life."[13] Later he says, "While you have the light, believe in the light, so that you may become children of light."[14] In Matthew, Jesus simply says to his disciples, "You are the light of the world."[15] Jesus is saying something about our true humanity, as he lives that humanity where it is found: in God. We, like Jesus, are the light of the world, when we, like Jesus, live in love with God.

Jesus speaks not only about himself, but about us, when he says, "Foxes have dens, and the birds in the sky have nests, but the Human One has no place to lay his head."[16] (I am using the Common English Bible translation here and in the following verses with its translation of the Aramaic idiom, υἱὸς τοῦ ἀνθρώπου ["Son of Man"], as "Human One.") Like Jesus, the Human One, our home is in God; it cannot be established here and now in the material of the world in and of itself. We cannot simply set up house here, but rather must remember that we are on a journey in response to the call and Spirit of God.

"The Human One has authority on the earth to forgive sins."[17] Jesus declares the same of his followers, "Truly I tell you, whatever you bind on earth will be bound in heaven, and whatever you loose on earth will be loosed in heaven."[18] "The Human One did not come to be served but rather to serve and to give his life to liberate many people."[19] Jesus lets his followers know that what is true for him is true for them. It is the way of God's reign and it contrasts with the way authority is exercised in the world. The authority we receive from God is authority to serve and liberate. "The greatest among you must become like a person of lower status and the leader like a servant."[20] This is divine reality and it is stamped upon our humanity. It is manifest when we are transformed from one degree of our true humanity to another.

There are, of course, many places in the synoptic gospels where "Son of Man" or "Human One" refers to Jesus' unique mission (his coming death

13. John 8:12.
14. John 12:36.
15. Matt 5:14.
16. Matt 8:20 (CEB).
17. Matt 9:6, (CEB).
18. Matt 18:18.
19. Matt 20:28.
20. Luke 22:26 (CEB).

and its meaning). However, Jesus makes clear that, even here, we participate in a common humanity with Jesus, for to be truly human in a world
that has lost its humanity means facing rejection. "They will arrest you and
persecute you; they will hand you over to synagogues and prisons, and you
will be brought before kings and governors because of my name."[21] There
are also apocalyptic sayings that refer to the Human One coming "with
the majesty of his Father with his angels" at the end of the age.[22] We do not
readily see ourselves in these sayings, except that we are gathered with Jesus
into the "age to come."

In the Gospel of John, where the divine shines forth in Jesus, we also
see our humanity as it comes to be in union with God. Can we not also say
with Jesus, as we come to be in God through Christ, "I and the Father are
one" and "if you have seen me, you have seen the Father"? We are to be
revelations of God through the one who is *the* revelation of God. We may
only get a taste of this, but it is a taste of being truly human as we find our
true selves in God through Christ Jesus.

There is a temptation to separate what is united in Jesus, to speak as
if Jesus' humanity is seen in his weeping at Lazarus's tomb and in his suffering and death, while Jesus' divinity is seen in his healings and miracles.
However, Jesus is not half human and half divine, but is the *union* of God
and humanity. In Jesus, the Human One, we encounter the divine; in his
weeping and brokenness, we recognize God's presence and power. And it
is the same for us who in Christ have become "participants in the divine
nature."[23] The divine is expressed in our humanity and God is one with his
creation.

We must see ourselves in Jesus, in his being and in his action—the
two cannot be separated. This means that a Christian and human praxis
cannot be understood apart from our being "in Christ," nor apart from the
activity of the Spirit of God. It also means that Jesus' life, as an example and
a mirror, makes concrete what the anointing of the Spirit produces—what
a truly Christian and human praxis looks like.

21. Luke 21:12.
22. Matt 16:27.
23. 2 Pet 1:4.

Dynamics of Discernment

It clearly is not enough to *know* what Jesus did. We must come to *live* the life "in Christ" and as such come to know this life from the inside. Furthermore, having a treasure store of Jesus' sayings and actions and biblical and theological knowledge, along with our own experiences from which we can draw as those trained for God's reign, is not enough to answer the question, "What now"? In the complexities of our present situations, with our sense of how Jesus operates, what are we to do? The problem is not simply that we live in a very different time and place, but that a number of possible choices often are available to choose from, any one of which we could argue are Jesus-like. Paul, who did live in Jesus' time, had to make decisions regarding next steps. At one point, when faced with various possible objectives for the mission, he was "forbidden by the Holy Spirit to speak the word in Asia." He received a vision in the night directing him to Macedonia, rather than Asia, and discerned that this vision was from God.[24] Paul's treasure of theology and past experiences did not by themselves provide the direction of his gospel mission.

We have a treasure store to draw from. Without the leading of the Spirit, however, we lose our way as individuals and as congregations. Our treasure store of knowledge, accumulated wisdom and experiences gives us the terrain; the Spirit helps us with our concrete decisions. Our awareness of the current situation and the sense we have of our mission (Jesus' mission) is often our main help, but sometimes we are faced with various possibilities for moving forward. In this case, we must choose. Making a choice matters. But the accumulated knowledge of the situation and our understanding of the mission does not get us there. There is a transcendental and practical aspect to our decision-making.

There is a practical logic of the Spirit, a dynamic of spiritual knowing, which opens up the way for concrete decisions that are fitted for our coming to be as individuals and for our mission as congregations. Karl Rahner refers to a "logic of concrete individual knowledge" that he finds described in Ignatius of Loyola's *Spiritual Exercises*.[25] It is a dynamic of practical knowing that we can recognize in our own experience of making decisions. We could call it the ordinary dynamic of spiritual direction and discernment. Even with the more extraordinary experience of a vision in

24. Acts 16:6–10.
25. Rahner, *Dynamic Element*, 84–170.

the night, Paul had to discern where the vision came from, by means of the "logic" of the Spirit.

In any given situation, as we face various possible courses of action, we make decisions based on whether or not a particular course of action "pleases" us. The experience of being pleased or the sense of fittingness is grounded in our fundamental stance in life. If our stance is with pleasure (seek pleasure, avoid pain), then what pleases us will be whatever gives pleasure. If our stance is anchored in faith and the love of God, then our experience of fittingness comes from within the horizons of that stance. In openness and response to the call of God, we find ourselves doing as Ignatius directs us, deciding and acting in peace rather than out of "desolation," discord, restlessness, or fear. In trust and openness to God, we make our journey in life by decisions that are in keeping with that trusting openness to God. We move in directions in which we are at peace. Rather than being driven into action by boredom or restlessness or pride or fear or unsettledness of one kind or another, we respond openly to the leading of the Spirit. We wait for the right time, speaking the word we recognize as fitting for the moment—or, we live in the silence that we experience as appropriate to the situation. Some courses of action can be dictated by our sense of what is appropriate for us as human beings; that is, dictated by our sense of the common humanity we all share. Other courses of action may be determined by our experience of what is appropriate to who we are as individuals or congregations; our own sense of individual or communal calling. Certainly, our history, theology, and morality—the ethical stands of our community and significant individuals—all go into our sense of what is appropriate action in each particular situation. Nevertheless, along with this landscape of our history and experience, we make decisions about what actions to take, and with each decision, we are saying something about what we believe it is to be human and what we believe God intends us to become and do *in this moment.*

In some cases, in surrendered openness to God, we perceive with a kind of immediacy or directness, the action that we must take. We perceive that *this* decision is right for this time and place and for who God is calling us to be, as God's people. At other times, we may go through a degree of struggle—even agonizing over decisions. We may need a time of testing to sort out the appropriateness of a particular decision. We may need to imagine ourselves in a concrete situation, to see in our mind's eye whether or not it is right for us. We are, of course, referring to actions that in principle are neither right nor wrong, but have to do with our own callings, whether as individuals or congregations. Are we to love this sister or brother by listening or by speaking a particular word of counsel? Or is the way of love, in this moment, silence and prayer? Imagination is God's gift for such times. We may imagine ourselves in a particular situation (in some cases we may even be able to try out the situation), to see if it seems fitting to who we are called to be and how we must act.

If we and our churches are going to be truly about the mission of the people of God, we must live by a sense of calling and make decisions by the leading of the Spirit. "For all who are led by the Spirit of God are children of God." The mission of the church and the ministry of its leaders exists by a sense of calling. It is for this reason that prayer is critical in the life of congregations and their leaders. Prayer, at its heart, is the turning of our hearts, emotions, will, and mind to God—the turning over of our lives to God. Prayer is the testing ground for our decisions. In prayer, pastors and congregations weigh the various possibilities before them (generally there are, in any given situation, only a limited number of possibilities that present themselves). In prayer, they bring the various possible actions before God in that infinite openness that reaches out for God. When the "what's in it for us" mindset gets in the way of that God-given openness, blocked by a finite object toward which our orientation has become misdirected, we sense the dissonance. Something has come between us and God; the way being presented to us is not one into which we are called. Where, rather than peace, we experience resistance or discord in our relation to God, we are likely sensing a decision that is not in response to the God who calls us into being. We may even discern that our motives are something other than a desire to serve God. Rather than the movement and motivation of faith and the love of God, there is the desire for self-gratification or self-promotion.

Our coming to a decision may involve varying degrees of ambiguity and confusion, depending on the kind of ulterior motives present and the difficulties of context and history. Nevertheless, Spirit-led decision-making is the means by which we, as individuals and communities of faith, move in the direction of our God-given callings. We cannot necessarily wait to make a decision until all ambiguity and confusion are resolved. Often we must "feel" our way in the direction of what we sense is fitting within a particular situation in spite of the dissonance and struggle. With "fear and trembling," we may at times follow the way of peace and a sense of fittingness.

It is clear that this spiritual dynamic of discerning concrete and timely actions is not necessarily without conflict or tension. We tend to talk ourselves into actions, to rationalize, to justify decisions formed by ulterior motives. The way of peace is the way of letting go of the clamor of voices that would call us aside from the activity to which the Spirit is leading. It is a matter of letting go, so that "God can do the talking," so that the Spirit can lead. There is no question that to go in the way of peace with God is to be in conflict with, in Paul's language, the "world and the flesh." Jesus, the Prince of Peace, said that he came not to make peace, but to bring a sword. In a world where humanity runs from its true self, the call to our true humanity creates tremendous conflict. This dynamic of discerning our true action, as children of God, places us in the midst of the battle.

On one occasion at St. Thomas, we were faced with a significant decision for a new ministry. We gathered our leadership together (leadership team, prayer ministers, deacons, and others) and sought God's guidance in prayer, being mindful of this spiritual dynamic being described. We prayed for some weeks with a commitment to wait for agreement in the Spirit, and came together periodically to share our thoughts. There were about a dozen of us; we relatively quickly came to a peace and consensus except for two of our group. In the process of sharing, it became very clear that, for these two individuals, there was considerable blockage in terms of "what was in it for them." And yet, it was difficult for them to recognize the extent to which their fears and issues were blurring their vision. As it was, there came a point where the door to this new ministry closed. We learned that making the commitment to consensus might not have been appropriate. The pastor and other leaders needed to move on with the general discernment. Nevertheless, we discovered the possibilities and power of praying together toward a decision.

This spiritual dynamic of recognizing that which needs to be said or done or acted upon contrasts with notions of decision-making as an act of drawing out the implications of Christian doctrines and principles. Certainly, Christian theology provides a backdrop for much Christian and churchly decision-making. However, all the Christian and human understanding that we can accumulate will not, in and of themselves, sustain the daily living out of our calling before God. There are always a number of possibilities; any one of these will not necessarily "break a commandment," but nevertheless can be the wrong action at a given time. We are, by necessity, by our human constitution, dependent upon God in all our moments for discerning what is fitting and right. As we act from that discernment, we come to be who God created us to be, and live out the mission to which we are called. Christian theology and ethics itself can only truly be understood as we live in the reality of faith and, therefore, by the leading of the Spirit. God's will being "done on earth as it is in heaven" is primarily and fundamentally an act of lived faith.

It is also an act of love: "You shall love the Lord your God with all your heart, and with all your soul, and with all your might."[26] It is this centering that makes us love what is pleasing to God. (As Augustine notes, "Love God and do what you please.") And it is also an act of hope. Hope discerns God's purposes, as it stretches out for the "always more" that God has for us. Hope reaches out towards God's future. It is not satisfied with the present perspectives or the present actions of love. It seeks to bring into being the "more" that God has for us, in our coming to be who God has created and liberated us to be. It is at the heart of the church's prophetic witness.

Prophetic Witness

Hope gives us the expansive horizons of God's future, in which we view the more immediate possibilities before us. Despair locks us into immediate circumstances and desires. Hope frees us to see beyond the immediate personal and social obstacles and barriers, as well as the desires and attitudes in the mixed bag of our conscious experience. It is like standing on a mountain and seeing before us the lay of the land, so that the immediate is not a wall that confines, but rather a revelation of the nearest possible opportunities before far-reaching horizons that beckon us on. Hope provides vision and purpose—it empowers us.

Frederick Douglass gives us one of the most powerful examples of hope that I have encountered. In his autobiography, he shares with us his relationship to an elderly black man, a man of wisdom, and the Spirit. For a period of time, Douglass, in his teens, would visit Uncle Lawson weekly. Uncle Lawson would counsel him and pray for him. In Douglass's words:

> He fanned my already intense love of knowledge into a flame by assuring me that I was to be a useful man in the world. When I would say to him, "How can these things be? and what can I do?" his simple reply was, "Trust in the Lord." When I would tell him, "I am a slave, and a slave for life, how can I do anything?" he would

26. Deut 6:5.

quietly answer, "The Lord can make you free, my dear; all things are possible with Him; only have faith in God. 'Ask, and it shall be given you.' If you want liberty, ask the Lord for it in faith, and he will give it to you."[27]

This word of hope remained with Douglass as he entered ever greater experiences of the brutality of the slave system, at times even despairing of life. The recurring thought "I am a slave for life" would itself drag him to despair. Yet, there was that other word of God's liberation that brought hope to his soul. It released him in the midst of impossible circumstances to take steps. To other slaves, he became an evangelist of that hope that was within. It was a dangerous evangelism, for he assured other slaves that the prevailing false religion that told them they were fitted by God to be slaves, that they were to obey their masters, was not from God but from the evil one. God was on their side. God was for their liberation. Of course, Douglass, acting on that hope and at great risk, got his liberty and became one of the greatest abolitionists in the fight against slavery.

Hope reaches beyond the circumstances to God's future, and therefore is integral to the dynamic of prophetic witness, for it frees us from the confines of the present situation. There is good reason why so much prophecy has a future element to it. While prophecy is essentially a word of God for the present situation and immediate future, it is directed nevertheless to the present as seen from God's future: the present seen before the expanse of God's end and goal for humankind. Christian hope looks toward the end that is the free reign of God's boundless love.

This dynamic of hope presses us past present obstacles and immediate goals toward God, who is the goal of human history. As we reach out for God, who is our future, we see the present and immediate future from the vantage point of a stretching out toward the end. We make our more immediate goals and decisions in a stretching out to God, who is the goal of goals. The Christian community whose head is Jesus, if it is to be true to itself, cannot escape this prophetic reality. We claim to follow the prophet of God's coming reign. Such a community can never be merely a preserver of past traditions, but must be a bearer of God's goal for humanity and creation. The goals and decisions that the Christian community makes must reflect the end toward which all things move. The church of Christ, if it is true to itself, must continually point the way, in its actions, toward this end.

27. Douglass, *Life and Times*, 45.

Living by hope means living by prayer and dependence on the Spirit of God. Next steps taken and next words spoken must often be determined not only by referring back to words formerly spoken, but by reaching out to the God of our future for what must be done or said now—in this moment—for our coming to be. Our past goals were good for the past and are continually overturned, not only by the realities of the present, but by the movement of history (our own and the human family's) to its end. Present goals are critiqued by that final goal to which we reach out. Christians have always known this: that no present reality can be embraced as the end and summing up of all things. Every present reality and decision of our lives must be overturned (and taken up into that which surpasses it), in light of the next step God calls us to take on our journey to the fullness of God's reign. Therefore, we must press on, declaring with Paul, "forgetting what lies behind and straining forward to what lies ahead, I press on toward the goal, for the prize of the heavenly call of God in Christ Jesus."[28]

This stretching out is itself the dynamic that perceives the new word that must be taken, the new action that must be done. What was said above concerning our decision-making by the leading of the Spirit (and therefore by faith) is now being expressed in a slightly different form. Deciding from a living trust in God is at the same time deciding before the future of God toward which we stretch. Hope does not allow us to be content or comfortable with our present decisions and actions. Hope knows there is always more. Hope, which stretches out for God, who alone is our future, causes us to see that our present reality always is incomplete. At no time can we stop and say, "This is it. I like it right here. I will stay and make this my life. I have all I need." To say, "Soul, you have ample goods laid up for many years; relax, eat, drink, be merry," is self-destruction.[29]

This is true for both individuals and communities of faith. The Christian community that Paul describes as the body of Christ cannot find its mission only in its traditions. The church that no longer hopes, which no longer finds its direction from the future, from the call of God in Christ, loses its way and is in danger of ceasing to be the church of Christ. Prophetic perception and witness therefore cannot exist without prayer understood as openness to God and God's future. A number of years ago, I heard a pastor declare that he had found a prophetic procedure for the church in community organizing principles. We delude ourselves. There are no

28. Phil 3:12–14.
29. Luke 12:19.

such principles for prophetic action. There is a dynamic that is inherent to our humanity, as God created and liberated us. It is a spiritual dynamic of prayer understood as surrendered openness to the promptings of God's Spirit, to the impressions of what is fitting for the next word or action in the present moment, before the expanse of God's future.

St. Thomas was heavily involved with faith-based community organizing. The principles for organizing were very human principles for effective meetings, leadership, and actions. They were great for organizing us. While faith-based, we invited any who shared our concerns for justice to participate. There were many allies who had no religious affiliation. The leadership, however, consisted primarily of clergy and people of faith. It was the reality of faith that gave to our actions a prophetic element, as experienced in prayers and vision, and in the words and actions directed to oppressive conditions.

Furthermore, people of faith understand the importance of *faithful* witness. It is a principle of community organizing to choose fights that can be won. Yet, we often did not win our winnable fights, or the compromises we made were such that calling it a win was a stretch. There were also the occasional actions that were like a gnat pestering an elephant. There was nothing that remotely looked winnable (certainly not in the short term— and not without momentous societal change). It was simply a matter of faithful witness to God's word and call. The Spirit will lead us in ways that defy our "organizing principles."

We who are the bearers of God's liberation are dependent upon the Spirit of God for timely, concrete, faithful witness in the world. We cannot be salt, light, and yeast in our world, except insofar as we live prophetically and prayerfully. If we are going to give witness to the reign of God as it is pressing in upon our world today, we must be actively stretching out for God's future in openness and faith, receptive to the call of God for this time and present situation. If we will not live in prayer and openness to the present purposes of God, doing and declaring those things that we perceive as fitting for this time and place, we will be irrelevant in the most radical sense. Ceasing to be the church, we will have become museums for the maintaining and observance of past documents and quaint religious (cultural) rituals, no longer appreciating their meaning or living in and by the power they once held.

The community of Jesus' followers lives by repentance and faith—by conversion from the idolatries of our world to the centering of its life in the living and active word of God. The witness and mission of the church of Christ moves forward by continually turning from the idolatries of the present age to "serve the living and true God." The church, in being true to itself, speaks and acts out that which it perceives as "fitting" in the present situation as it, living under God's reign, is open to the call of God. We walk not by sight (by the ready-to-hand confessions of the past, abstract theological principles or moral dictums formed by a present-day ethical casuistry), but by radical dependence upon the living God for the new word, direction, and witness within the configurations of the present situation.

People Who Belong to the Way

Given the foregoing, it should not surprise us that the *ecclesia* of God, in its beginnings, was called "the people who belonged to the Way." We are who we are because we are united to Jesus Christ the Way and have come to be a people led by the Spirit of God. Everything about us ought to exude this reality.

Jesus is anointed with the Spirit at the river Jordan. After his victory over the temptations in the wilderness, he immediately begins his ministry. Jesus is empowered by the Spirit of God and sent out to proclaim the good news of God's coming reign, to heal, deliver, and die as a ransom for many. The book of Acts gives a similar narrative of the early church. On the Day of Pentecost, the Holy Spirit is poured out on the gathered disciples, who immediately proclaim the good news of God's reign and victory. Peter declares God's deliverance: God raised the crucified Jesus from the dead. "God has made him both Lord and Messiah, this Jesus whom you crucified." As Jesus proclaimed repentance at the breaking in of God's reign, so does Peter: "Repent, and be baptized every one of you in the name of Jesus Christ so that your sins may be forgiven; and you will receive the gift of the Holy Spirit."[30]

In chapter 1 of Acts, the disciples are waiting for the Spirit. In chapter 2, the Spirit is poured out. In chapter 3, Peter and John, in the name of Jesus, heal a man lame from birth and proclaim the good news to a gathered crowd. In chapter 4, they are arrested and brought before the council in Jerusalem and ordered to no longer speak or teach in the name of Jesus. Their answer: "Whether it is right in God's sight to listen to you rather than

30. Acts 2.

to God, you must judge; for we cannot keep from speaking about what we have seen and heard."[31]

The pattern continues throughout Acts: proclamation, healings, deliverance from spiritual powers, and contending with those in authority—along with prayer meetings and the reality of gathered communities of those who "belonged to the Way."[32] This was the remembered praxis of these early followers of Jesus. It is significant that these believers were related to "the Way." They "had been instructed in the Way of the Lord."[33] There were those who refused to believe who "spoke evil of the Way."[34] When Paul was brought before Felix, governor of Judea, he connects himself to "the Way," which he says "some call a sect."[35] Paul says he worships the God of his ancestors "according to the Way." It is not according to a particular form of dogmatic theology, but according to the Way. We get a feel for the priority of praxis over theoria.

But it is the praxis of the Spirit fleshed out in acts of serving directed to healing and to our being liberated into life in God and in the community created by the Spirit. This is a praxis that flows from congregations filled with the Spirit, alive to the impressions of the Spirit, open to and anticipating God's action and expecting God's direction. The form God's guidance takes is always that of compassionate serving and speaking the truth in love. It is also a serving with authority—with the authority and power of the Spirit. Therefore, there is a ministry of healing in these congregations. There is deliverance from addictions and various powers that hold sway over us.

This authority and liberating work is born from our weakness, helplessness, and desperate need for God. In our weakness, Christ is strong.[36] This is seen in Paul's going to Corinth in "weakness and in fear and in much trembling," fearful after many beatings and imprisonments, but going anyway.[37]

> But we have this treasure in clay jars, so that it may be made clear that this extraordinary power belongs to God and does not come

31. Acts 4:9–10.

32. Acts 9:2.

33. Acts 18:25.

34. Acts 19:9.

35. Acts 24:14.

36. 2 Cor 12:10.

37. 1 Cor 2:3.

from us. We are afflicted in every way, but not crushed; perplexed, but not driven to despair; persecuted, but not forsaken; struck down, but not destroyed; always carrying in the body the death of Jesus, so that the life of Jesus may also be made visible in our bodies.[38]

Paul proclaims, from his experience, a "Christ crucified" who, for those called, is "the power of God and the wisdom of God." It is in our weakness and broken condition that we receive this message and God's strength.

What keeps us from this Spirit-praxis is our controlling ways, dependence on our theological acumen and our ability to apply it, and in our general tendency to be strong in ourselves. (I suspect others have the same experience that I have.) I believe I am more or less quoting Rahner when I write that our independence is in direct proportion to our dependence on God. Our freedom in the Spirit and openness to the Spirit rests in accepting our helplessness and our need of God.

We are being called back to our original identity as people of the Way, who are utterly dependent on God for the way in which to walk. As we consider evangelism in the time in which we live, certainly we can see that the only way to engage others is through the weakness that knows God's power. And in the Spirit who leads. As such, we meet others who, as human beings, have spiritual experience in some form or another. They are somewhere on a journey or fighting the journey, fighting the Way. We meet them not with answers and doctrines, but at the point where they are on their journey, which calls from us spiritual discernment and openness. It is as people of the Way that we can engage people of other faiths (and people of no explicit faith) and share from our experience into theirs, as we are open to theirs.

It is from our experience that we also can address the addictions and idols of our time. We can speak against that which has us bound and demeans our humanity—that which keeps us from our true selves created for love.

Contending With Authorities

One of the striking aspects of the people who belonged to the Way in the book of Acts, is the prevalence of contention with authorities. Peter and John are brought before the council; apostles are arrested by the high priest,

38. 2 Cor 4:7–10.

imprisoned, and flogged; Stephen is arrested, brought before the council, and executed; James is killed by King Herod and Peter is imprisoned; Paul and Silas are beaten in Philippi; Paul is brought before the council; Paul is brought before Felix the governor; Paul is brought before Festus; Paul is brought before Agrippa.[39] Often the conflict began with the populace and then leaders intervened. Among Jewish leaders in Jerusalem, the issue was the subversion of law and traditions and the undermining of leaders' authority. In the Jewish diaspora, there was the additional concern of potential converts, Gentile "God-fearers," being stolen by this sect of the Way. In the Greco-Roman world, the issues revolved around the authority of gods and emperor and related way of life.

Paul's encounter with the artisans of Artemis and those who sold images of the goddess is telling in this regard.[40] Paul's call to turn from idols was causing economic distress, as people turned from the goddess Artemis. Acts calls it a "great disturbance about the Way." The disturbance was religious, political, and economic (these are after all, intertwined). But it was the economic effect that really got things stirred up. Business was down when it came to selling silver shrines of the goddess Artemis. It was affecting the sellers, the skilled craftsmen, and the workers in related trades. The message of those who belonged to the Way was dangerous: "There is danger not only that our trade will lose its good name, but also that the temple of the great goddess Artemis will be discredited; and the goddess herself, who is worshiped throughout the province of Asia and the world, will be robbed of her divine majesty."[41] Their reaction can be summed up with the words, "Don't you dare touch my god!" "Don't you talk about my god!" ("Don't bring it up in a sermon!")

The situation is no different today in these United States of America. We have idols that are deeply embedded in the fabric of our society. Why do many pastors have difficulty talking about money and its place in our lives, doing so in concrete, specific ways, addressing the various aspects of our materialism? We know it is a touchy subject. It is an idol. Why do many have difficulty speaking against war and our warring ways? It is a touchy subject, because militarism and our security are idols. Why is race such a difficult subject (especially among white people)? It is because racism, the idolatry of "my people," is a part of the atmosphere we breathe. It is so

39. Acts 4:1–21, 5:17–39, 6:8–7:60, 12:15, 23:1–11, 24:1–27, 25:1–12, 26.

40. Acts 19:23–41.

41. Acts 19:27.

inculcated into our consciousness and shared experience that it is difficult to identify. Some will say that they are touchy on this subject because of fear of incrimination or being judged. But that is also idolatry—our appearance and image before others.

As members of St. Thomas became more aware of their neediness and became willing to share from their place of brokenness, our community prayer time on Sundays became, at times, simply confession. Sometimes those new to our fellowship found it a little disconcerting. James writes, "Confess your sins to one another."[42] There was a period in our congregation's history where we simply moved into this experience.

It is only as the *ecclesia* of God confesses and is liberated from its idols that we become witnesses before the world and that our witness becomes a disturbance (at which point, it is seen as subversive). As we are being set free and our lifestyles and priorities are being subverted under God's reign, that which we live for and value will make some uncomfortable. And when we speak truth to power, there will be a disturbance. In the political arena, we will speak from our experience of God's governance. Politics no longer can be separated off from the exercise of our faith. The church and its representatives must speak with one voice to the issues that a discerning church sees, not merely the issues the world sees. Bishops must represent the church in speaking to issues in the area of their jurisdiction. And we must *do* the truth as people of the Way.

It may be that it is time to bring back that phrase, "people of the Way." What if we regularly identified ourselves with those words as congregations? We are a people called to concrete practical action, activated by the Spirit and conforming to Jesus, who is the Way. A church that spoke with one voice and embodied action would be an example to the world of what the Way looks like.

42. Jas 5:16.

7

Worship

Where the Spirit of the Lord is, there is freedom. (2 Cor 3:17)

PAUL REFERS TO OUR being freed from the veil that has been over our minds, so that "with unveiled faces . . . [we] are being transformed . . . from one degree of glory to another."[1] The freedom that is ours in the presence of the Spirit brings transformation. We move from one form to another as we take on the image of God. In their historical context, these words are being read to a gathered community of believers, for whom the reality of the Spirit and the Spirit's gifts are celebrated. (These gifts are significant enough to be a source of dissension as the "flesh" kicks in with comparisons and competition.) Above all, it is by the Spirit that the Corinthian church, gathered for worship, is being liberated "from one degree of glory to another."

For the gathered community of the Spirit there is freedom. There is freedom to worship. There is freedom for the word. There is freedom to receive. There is freedom for the ministry of liberation. There is freedom for the sending, with power, to do the work of liberation.

Freedom to Worship

Leo Tolstoy, in his novel, *Resurrection*, depicts two types of worship, Orthodox ritual and Evangelical sentiment. The Orthodox service takes place in a prison with liturgy and prayers read by a priest, with words distant from the lived reality of the participants and the beliefs of the priest—words like

1. 2 Cor 3:18.

96

"mother of God" and "flesh of God." The belief of the participants moved along the lines of magic. Prisoners hoped, by participating in the ritual, that they would gain favor with God for changes in their situation. Prison guards hoped for God's co-signing their brutality. At the Evangelical meeting, in a house of a very wealthy family with their friends, we are given another depiction of worship. The tears and smiles of the preacher were produced at the appropriate points in his sermon, to gain the greatest impact. The message of God's wrath against human sin, which brought tears, was followed by the good news of God's Son, the stand-in for our punishment, a proclamation that left in bondage the wealthy participants, brought no relief to the abject poor and left in place the great economic inequality of Russia in the late nineteenth century.[2]

It is not difficult to recognize similar forms of worship in our own time and culture—forms that are experienced with little change and liberation for participants. For some, worship is a common ritual that often operates like an empty vessel, to be filled with the meaning that is brought to it by those engaged. Rather than a word that calls those gathered to a changed life, it merely holds the desires and agendas of the participants. For others, worship consists of emotional words, sentiment, and music, which provide good feelings for their return home, and the thought that God will prosper them. Worship in some form or fashion is felt to put God on our side, but with little liberation and transformation of our lives. (What do people with little experience of Christians see when they turn on a television channel where "evangelicalism" is a combination of a satisfaction theory of atonement and nationalist societal values, or where God prospering us looks a lot like a materialist "American dream"?)

For those who gather where the historic liturgy is used, or where there is strong content in the structure of worship, the challenge of gospel worship may be there, but the content has to be understood. And understanding does not only have to do with making the words more contemporary. There has to be an openness to the words, a desire to worship and submission to the leading of the Spirit.

It has been noted that liturgy (*leitourgia*) means "work of the people." But prior to a work or expression of the people in a form of worship, there is the work of the Spirit in liberating us *from* the worship of ourselves, *to* the worship of God.

2. Tolstoy, *Resurrection*, 138–41, 271–73.

Before St. Thomas was an African-American congregation, it was a white congregation—and then an integrated congregation. When I came to St. Thomas, it was an African-American congregation using a very Euro-centric hymnal. The liturgy was not worn comfortably. We began making simple changes using an African-American hymnal, and making changes to the music of the liturgy. The service became more "comfortable" and available to visitors, but our worship only deepened as we became increasingly open to the Spirit.

There were events in our life and worship—loss of resources, change in the way we thought of ourselves—that threw us upon God's mercy. We found ourselves calling out to God for help. Without our former choir and musicians, without keyboard and drums, but with a small worship team, we turned to the Holy Spirit to lead us into worship—the same Spirit that was releasing us outward and freeing us for ministry. Our worship became freer and more real. Members began asking for change in our liturgy in order to align with who we were becoming in worship and ministry. In the Lutheran hymnal at that time, there were rubrics that prescribed various elements of the liturgy with the words "may" or "shall." We realized that we were going to have to address not only the "mays," but the "shalls." The acknowledgment that "where the Spirit of the Lord is, there is freedom" was the way forward. The "historical liturgy" remained in skeletal form, but was stamped with the expression of God's people in that place and with space for spiritual movement and the ministry of liberation and healing.

Ministry in Worship

The ministry of liberation starts in worship; it moves from the center of a congregation's life and mission. It does not start with an abstraction, an idea or a form, but with submission to God. It is the work of the Spirit and therefore of freedom. Worship in Spirit and in truth liberates. It releases outward. The deliverance experienced in the gathered community in worship moves out to the world where the gathered are sent.

The gifts of the Spirit, exercised within the gathering of believers, are gifts for liberation. The gift of mercy welcomes those bound, burdened, and oppressed. The gift of prophecy proclaims a timely message directed to the needs present and calls for response and action to the vision God provides. The gift of organizing helps put the communal vision into action. The gift of healing extends God's deliverance by connecting the power of

God to restoration of body, soul, and spirit. The gift of the gospel offers God's liberation as a gift. The gift of teaching provides understanding of God's liberating work, as well as wisdom for our earthly journey and mission in the world. The pastoral gift shepherds those being released in order that each may receive and use his or her gifts in the work of God's liberating reign. The great variety of spiritual gifts equip the community of faith for the varied ministry of liberation. These gifts are all expressions of the foundational gifts of Word and Spirit—the Word proclaimed and lived, and the Spirit empowering.

For these gifts of liberation to be exercised, there has to be space provided within the gatherings of God's people, especially at worship. At St. Thomas we found that we had to make space for singing songs of praise, for community prayer, and for prayer ministry teams at the eucharistic feast. Community prayer, especially, was a time for the gathered people of God to minister to one another, and this could take many forms. It was sacred space for God's liberating work. ("For freedom Christ has set us free.") Freedom in Christ is always a freedom directed outward. The ministry that liberates us releases us into a ministry of liberation in relation to others.

This ministry is a ministry "in the Spirit," a praying in the Spirit, being led by the Spirit. Given the general condition of churches in these United States of America, we have to take up a conversation we have not had—a conversation with the Spirit. Talk about the Spirit. Take up the language of Scripture and seek understanding. Be open to the Spirit. Ask for the Spirit—"If you then, who are evil, know how to give good gifts to your children, how much more will the heavenly Father give the Holy Spirit to those who ask him!"[3]

The worship of some churches can be described as intellectual; others, emotional. In either case, worship is expressive of the human soul, but not necessarily of the divine Spirit. *Our* resources are noticeably present; not so with God's. The way out of this void begins with seeking, waiting, asking for the Spirit, letting others pray for us, and expecting a journey out of the denial of our condition. It entails an acknowledgment of our need and a turning from dependence upon ourselves to openness and submission to the Spirit of God—all of which we will come to recognize as the work of the Spirit and of God's grace. It is God who liberates.

We get an indication of this activity of the Spirit as a movement from denial to liberation in the Gospel of John. The Spirit convinces us of our

3. Luke 11:13

inturned condition and alienation from God and reveals God's justice and God's deliverance "because the ruler of this world has been condemned."[4] There is liberation from the forces that have kept us from our true selves and our true work.

We are liberated into a way of life, a praxis of the Spirit. The Spirit guides us into the truth and provides vision for what God is doing and is about to do. (The Spirit "will declare to you the things that are to come."[5]) Community worship, where gifts of the Spirit are present, is the central activity for guidance into truth and for the prophetic word that gives direction for next steps and for the church's missional vision. Worship in Spirit and in truth is anticipatory and filled with expectation. What will God say and do among us today, and for the sake of our movement outward, in the coming days?

Understood in this way, worship breaks up ideological idolatries of the right and the left. It is not ideology that directs our steps, but God, who is the source of our vision and action. The timely word and call to action will often surprise our personal ideologies and agendas. God's movement forward will be one of health and wholeness, filled with compassion, justice, and mercy.

Ministry of the Word

The Word of God comes to the gathered community in proclamation and incarnation, in the body of Christ, the sacraments and the gifts of the Spirit. Of special importance is the sermon, where scriptural interpretation within the context of the congregation and the world, with the help of the Spirit, makes God's word present and calls for response. In a sermon preached in London in 1933, Bonhoeffer said of the sermon: "When a preacher opens the Bible and interprets the word of God, a mystery takes place, a miracle: the grace of God, who comes down from heaven into our midst and speaks to us, knocks on our door, asks questions, warns us, puts pressure on us,

---

4. John 16:8–11: "And when he comes, he will prove the world wrong about sin and righteousness and judgment: about sin, because they do not believe in me; about righteousness, because I am going to the Father and you will see me no longer; about judgment, because the ruler of this world has been condemned."

5. John 16:13.

alarms us, threatens us and makes us joyful again, and free, and certain."[6] The sermon, when it is the word of God, changes and liberates.

A sermon that merely reflects from a place of self-satisfaction with our lives, our thoughts, and our feelings about God, while avoiding the challenge of God's word, leaves us in bondage. The word that sets us free is the word of God, which cuts to the innermost parts of our being, revealing the thoughts and intentions of our hearts.[7] It calls us out from where we hide, unmasking our false selves, our wayward living, the attitudes behind our thoughts about others, our idolatries and addictions that drive our words and actions.

The word of God addresses us where we live in the multiple contexts of our lives. Because it addresses us at the point of our idols and our temptations to idolatry, it calls us to faith and obedience. It lets us know that we cannot serve two masters. We have decisions of ultimate concern to make. This word is not merely about moral reform or about being better Christians; it is about to whom we belong and where we place our trust. Racism, for example, is not merely a wrong that must be corrected, it is an idol from which we must turn. It is the idolatry of ourselves and our group; change only happens as we confess, repent, and turn to God for our liberation. The word of God, therefore, comes with a call for response and reminds us that the Spirit will help us, that God is gracious, and that, with God, liberation is a gift.

The sermon is clearly critical for the gathered people of God in worship. When the sermon is heard as the word of God, it brings forth faith and deliverance, hope and healing. It calls forth the response of faith and obedience. If there is no faithful response to this call, then the word is rejected and a person remains bound in their idolatry. If there is no response, negative *or* positive, then it is likely that the word of God was not proclaimed or was not heard. The task of preaching demands the help of the Spirit to discern the word for the people of God gathered at a given time in the contexts in which they live, so that they receive a clear and piercing call. The Word ministers liberation.

---

6. Bonhoeffer, *Collected Sermons*, 90.

7. Heb 4:12–13: "Indeed, the word of God is living and active, sharper than any two-edged sword, piercing until it divides soul from spirit, joints from marrow; it is able to judge the thoughts and intentions of the heart. And before him no creature is hidden, but all are naked and laid bare to the eyes of the one to whom we must render an account."

Since God's word calls forth response (repentance, faith, obedience, thanksgiving, praise), the sermon must move toward and expect response. If there is little or no call for response, the sermon may be more a mild reflection on life than a word of God. Because the word calls for response, the liturgy can provide opportunities for various kinds of response. These calls for response can be calls that bring participants out of their seats ("altar calls"), calls to discipleship and commitment, calls to specific outreach ministries of the congregation, calls to specific social justice actions, calls to prayer, opportunities for personal ministry, for healing. Making prayer teams available provides ministry to individuals who respond to the word. In small congregations, individuals seeking prayer can gather in the center of the congregation and the community can pray for them, or people can gather in small groups to pray for each others' needs. In some denominational liturgies, a hymn and creed follow the word. The creed, a late addition to the historic liturgy, seems a poor response, a general and cerebral response. We can let the word determine the type of specific response, but generally let the response be sung and move into community prayer. Give the time necessary for the word and for prayer. People who have not been used to praying aloud with others can—and will—learn, given the opportunity to respond with prayer.

Response to the word is always a release outward for individuals and congregations. There are outward directed ministries and actions to which a congregation as a whole becomes committed, all members recognizing its common vision with its concrete implementations. Members of St. Thomas embraced a common commitment to recovery ministry, to ministry to neighborhood children and their families, to evangelizing our neighbors and to social justice actions, through a faith-based community organization. There were various kinds of personal involvement, depending on individuals' gifts and callings and where they were in their spiritual journey. There was, however, a common commitment to pray for and support these ministries. The call for response to the outward call of God carried with it these tangible realities of our life and mission.

Furthermore, when the word speaks to the wider context of our lives, beyond personal relationships, the liberating work of God to which we are called becomes increasingly holistic. It has us in a ministry of deliverance that combines body, soul, and spirit, family relationships, friends and acquaintances, neighbors, enemies, community, institutions, the body politic, national and global issues, hunger, environment, and future generations.

When the word is declared in this wider context, we respond with a wider ministry of liberation, as we are being released from that which binds us.

Ministry of Sacrament

Baptism is a gracious and powerful sign of God's liberating work. So, how do people who have a largely cultural relation to this sacrament come to experience its power? We have to recapture and communicate the reality that we go to baptism to *die*. We go to die so that we can also be raised alive to God and to God's will. If we have no intention to die (or bring our infant child to die), then baptism is not for us—at least not yet. When St. Thomas committed itself to reaching out to those who were not in a community of faith or had little or no experience with assemblies of God, we found that we were mostly baptizing adults and youth (few infants). Those coming for baptism came already experiencing a dying and rising in their lives, a repenting and believing that was releasing them into the life God gives. They were coming to desire the dying and rising that baptism represented and imparted, and the sign of the cross upon their lives. Baptism was one piece with the word they were hearing and the meaning of the fellowship into which they were being incorporated. Baptism was liberating *because* of the dying and rising. For those who came into the fellowship who had been baptized in their youth, but who had left the reality of their baptism far behind them, we provided a renewal of baptism, focusing on the dying and rising.

The symbol of baptism is made more tangibly expressed when immersion is used. Though not generally practiced in my denomination, I imagine there has been some revival of this method. I know of at least one Lutheran congregation on Chicago's south side that baptizes by immersion. At St. Thomas, on a few occasions, we also did so with youth (once on an early Sunday morning in Lake Michigan, and on another occasion in a wading pool set up at the church). The imagery and experience expresses the reality of a spiritual "drowning," necessary for rebirth, of the old life and the false self. Rising up out of the water tangibly gives feeling to our liberation to new life in Christ.

There is another aspect of baptism that is integral to our liberation: the anointing of the Spirit. Baptism into Christ is baptism with the Holy Spirit. The sacrament of baptism calls forth the pouring out of the Spirit, the sign of the Spirit's anointing expressed in the anointing with oil. Those baptized, who have come to the place of baptism drawn by the Spirit, can be encouraged to expect, wait upon and receive the empowering of the Spirit. By the power of God, they are being freed from the power of idolatry, addiction, and obsession, and they are being empowered for the ministry of liberation, in its many forms, with the gifts the Spirit gives.

It is critical that baptismal liturgies give expression to God's liberation. It is too easy for participants, given the middle-class-values legacy of many churches, to water down our "cleansing from sin" and our salvation to eternal life, to understand this ritual as being related to when we die sometime in the future. Those who come for baptism (and those who bring their children) need to hear the words of liberation from bondage through dying in the *present*, that we might also rise in the present, liberated for a ministry that sets captives free in all dimensions of human life. When baptisms carry the weight of these words and actions, the congregation is reminded of what it is liberated *from* and *for*.

The eucharist is a weekly reminder of the night in which Jesus Christ was betrayed. It is a reminder of his entrance into our suffering, and that, in him, we can take up our suffering and follow him. It gives expression within worship to our lived experience, to our broken selves and our solidarity with other broken selves. It gives expression to our broken community and society. It places us with Jesus, who did not avoid the cup God called him to drink, but rather took up his cross. His life was not merely taken from him; he gave it up. As we are called to the table of thanksgiving, we are called into communion with Christ along with all the saints, into a suffering world with the gospel of liberation in word and action.

The reality that we seek to avoid—but cannot—by escape into addictions, is the reality into which we are released through Christ. We take this life in, a body broken for us and blood shed for us. We live from this reality. We are freed to take up our cross. We enter the cross-bearing life, no longer committed to running from our suffering or that of others. We are, over and over again, Sunday after Sunday, released outward to a hurting world, to lose our lives for the sake of Christ and the gospel, as bearers of God's liberation. The form that liberation takes is related to the form of bondage we encounter, but always with the faithfulness, mercy, and justice that we receive when we consume Christ.

The Sending

The experience of being sent is in the freedom for which Christ has set us free. We are being released outward. This outward movement is becoming integral to our identity. We are apostles; we are the sent. Previously, we were entrenched in self-satisfaction or despair, but now we are freed to go and make disciples of all people. We are freed to serve. In worship, we are renewed and deepened by being sent.

We gather as sent people. Our experience of being sent into the world is there from the beginning of our gathering as a worshipping community. It is in the worship in which we glorify God and submit to God's will. The sending is in the general confession of sin at the beginning of the service, or during community prayer when God's people may get specific about their sins, refusing to remain in denial. It is an element in the response to the word, in repenting and allowing God to release us from addictions, in order to do God's will. It may be in the announcements when community members are lifting up movement issues and actions. It is in the eucharist, the fellowship, and the word; it is in all that empowers and sustains us for outward mission.

Along with the final "Go in peace and serve the Lord," we may include aspects of the congregation's mission. Feed someone who is hungry this week. Share the good news. "Carry this message to addicts (*Twelfth Step*)." Be faithful in doing justice and showing mercy. Be light in the darkness. Do the work of liberation.

8

Leadership

> For Christ did not send me to baptize but to proclaim the gospel,
> and not with eloquent wisdom, so that the cross of Christ might
> not be emptied of its power. (1 Cor 1:17)

PASTORS IN THE BODY of Christ, in their office and calling, are given the task of passing on to the people of God the simple gospel of the cross, where the power and wisdom of God reside. God comes to us in our weakness and failure, in our victimization and hurt, and the God who raised Jesus from the dead raises us to life in him, liberating us and making us "more than conquerors through him who loved us."[1] In his letters, Paul keeps bringing the church back to this central reality. Our liberation is not found in a particular group, ethnicity, or class: "I appeal to you, brothers and sisters, by the name of our Lord Jesus Christ, that all of you be in agreement and that there be no divisions among you, but that you be united in the same mind and the same purpose."[2] Our liberation is not found in the person or personality of the pastor or leader ("Was Paul crucified for you? Or were you baptized in the name of Paul?")[3] It is not found in our attempts at being and acting Christian ("Did you receive the Spirit by doing the works of the law or by believing what you heard?")[4] It is in the good news of the one who has

---

1. Rom 8:37.
2. 1 Cor 1:10.
3. 1 Cor 1:13.
4. Gal 3:2.

died for us, that in him we might die to a life turned in upon ourselves and rise alive to God and to God's will. It is God, in Christ, who is liberating us.

Those who are called to proclaim this gospel declare it to people in various states of readiness. Like seed being thrown out, the word may immediately be snatched away, or fall on stony ground, unable to take root, or be choked by the weeds of other commitments and cares, or fall on good soil, taking root and bearing fruit. The good news of God's reign cannot be made to fit our lifestyles, so that all will be happy to receive it as an add-on to those lifestyles. The word is good news for those who no longer have anywhere else to go, nothing else to lean on—who know they need God; they need God's forgiveness and deliverance. For those who trust in themselves and justify their actions, who have other commitments that they are unwilling to be loosed from, the good news sounds like *bad* news, for it implies that they have got it wrong. They would have to undergo a radical change. They would just as soon acknowledge that, yes, they get some things wrong and they could do better, but things are not that bad. But God's word and Spirit always come to let us know that things are worse than we think. Our condition is past our fixing. Only God can make things right—and has done so in Jesus Christ's dying and rising.

Ultimately, the issue is who or what reigns in our lives. The coming of God's reign can sound good to us until we realize that it means letting go of that which presently rules. We do not let God deliver us from our addiction (or idolatry) until we are willing for it to go. Until then, we simply are closed to what God is saying to us. We do not get anything from God's word; or we take bits and pieces from a sermon that we think will be useful to our present commitments. What we have assembled from the sermon parts, however, will no longer be God's word nor good news. The good news of God's reign being near becomes bad news when we have decided to remain on the outside. Therefore, the word remains, "*Repent*, and believe in the good news."[5] Pastors and proclaimers must steadfastly name the idols and addictions and call for a "return to the Lord, your God."

One of the temptations for pastors is to fix or soften the word of God and rob it of its power. This is true not only of the publicly proclaimed word, but of its extension in personal and spiritual counsel. Often people come to pastors looking for advice, when what we have to give is God's word of liberation. Often the advice or help sought from a pastor is characterized by commitments, apart from God, that the person would like the pastor to

5. Mark 1:14–15.

co-sign. "Teacher, tell my brother to divide the family inheritance with me." On the face of it, this sounds like a plea to a spiritual teacher to use his authority (leverage) to bring about a just transaction. However, Jesus does not allow himself to be put in that position. "Friend, who set me to be a judge or arbitrator over you?" Instead, Jesus addresses him and those present with the call to turn from anything that would take the place of God. "Take care! Be on your guard against all kinds of greed; for one's life does not consist in the abundance of possessions."[6]

God's grace is present for our liberation from false dependency. It provides nothing for maintaining our idolatry. It does not provide a general acceptance of or cover for our disobedience to God or our refusal to surrender that aspect of our lives that we steadfastly withhold from God. If we use grace in this way, as Bonhoeffer puts it, "The grace of God becomes, in the end, reduced to the grace I grant to myself."[7]

I learned to say to those who came to me for counsel that I was a spiritual counselor. Of course, I did not disregard the importance of psychology for understanding the person who came to me. Psychological factors form part of the interior landscape of the person (and sociological factors, the external), but my focus was on their spiritual journey, on what God was doing. Whether the concern was sin or suffering, an uneasy conscience or hurt, relationship problems or discerning God's will, the question was this: What is God saying? The way forward was through listening—listening to the person and to the Spirit. Prayer was critical, as well as was the awareness that what God was saying could come through the person counseled as well as the pastor.

When there is blockage and an inability to hear God's word or to receive forgiveness, when a person is stuck, refusing to submit to God's will, the word is a call to repentance in relation to a specific sin or idol. It is never about something general. There is a concrete issue that the Spirit moves to the forefront of a person's life. This issue demands a relinquishing and deliverance. When it begins to be named, we can expect pushback, for we are touching upon an idol. Bonhoeffer makes the point that "when no argument arises we should probably be afraid we've spoken only human counsel instead of God's word."[8] God's word calls forth our liberation. And it is this word that must be proclaimed, in many different ways, so that the

---

6. Luke 12:13–15.

7. Bonhoeffer, *Spiritual Care*, 33.

8. Ibid., 35.

hearers of the word may continue to move into the freedom for which God sets us free.

The release outward for congregations is rooted in this fundamental ministry to individuals, through the proclaimed word and spiritual counsel. The fundamental call for pastors is to proclaim, "Repent and have faith, for the reign of God is near," making this word specific, naming the idols that must be repented. People who repent and are liberated are free to give their lives for others. They come to share in the twofold ministry mentioned earlier in which Jesus addresses *both* oppressor and oppressed. The ministry of liberation is twofold! It comes to release us from oppressing and oppression.

If our focus as leaders is *solely* on the fight for social justice (addressing oppressive forces), without attending to our own personal liberation, we will end up walking over individuals as useful means to an end. Our own unacknowledged oppressive attitudes and ways will blind us to the needs of others. We may end up with an ideology rooted in self-righteousness and disdain for those we oppose, and insensitivity to the vulnerabilities of those whom we use to achieve our goals. On the other hand, if our focus is *solely* on a narrow personal and familial liberation, without addressing the wider affect of our addictions in producing social injustice, then we will end up with individuals and congregations that are turned in upon their personal piety. They work on themselves and their relationships, while remaining blind to the wider circles of oppression and oppressing and their own complicity. We are under call to proclaim a word and to provide counsel for ever-widening circles of liberation.

For those entering into the reality of repenting and trusting, dying and rising, the word addresses our maturation. It embraces dying and rising as a way of life. It speaks to people hungry to grow in this new reality. It speaks to temptations and trials, to pitfalls and barriers. It offers guidance for living from our source. Like those encouraging runners in a race, it supports and inspires. It calls God's people forward, providing vision and a future with hope.

Pastors, of course, are not the only ones who are bearers of the word and spiritual counselors of liberation. Pastors can identify others in their congregations who are being liberated and have a spiritual sense of what is at stake. Among them, there are those who have the spiritual discernment to be midwives at the spiritual birth of individuals—to be helpers on the journey of liberation. They also can act as shepherds for those coming into faith and freedom.

Training Leaders

Lay leaders can be recognized, nurtured, and trained. Lutheran pastors on Chicago's south side developed a two-year course for training deacons as servant leaders for our congregations. This diaconal training has included theology, biblical interpretation, church history, discipleship, prayer, prophetic witness, community organizing, and various kinds of ministry to the sick, grieving, addicted, abused, and imprisoned. At its foundation, it is a training in a ministry of the word and Spirit. As we see it, God is raising up partners in the gospel of liberation.

The training of lay leaders must be contextual and structured by the needs of the congregation and community, as well as by the gifts of the leaders. What are the needs of the community? What kinds of liberation are needed? What are the gifts and callings of the leaders being sent out? Training is directed to the formation of servant leaders ministering in the world and to building up the body of Christ for the outward mission of the church.

Foundational to training lay leaders is the example of Jesus. Potential leaders need to have placed before them the particularity of Jesus as a "model of the godly life." In getting a sense of Jesus, in the concrete historical situation of his time, his humanity becomes real. One of our diaconal students expressed elation at encountering Jesus as an actual historical figure in all his uniqueness, rather than, as he expressed it, a kind of metaphor. Receiving a fresh understanding of Jesus and his teaching and lifestyle brings a flesh and blood reality to what many in our pews experience as fuzzy or confusing. Jesus is often encased in doctrinal language that distances church members from the lived reality. The more they can see their true humanity in him, the more their own lives are critiqued and a radically alternate lifestyle called forth.

Along with Jesus' particularity, leaders can be encouragement by the reality of our being baptized into, and participating in, Christ. Our growth in Christ is always Christ being formed in us, by the power of the Spirit. Help with prayer, praying in the Spirit, (or "contemplative prayer") and being led by the Spirit are critical. Our individual callings and the mission of the church is a movement of the Spirit. *Koinonia* (fellowship), small group sharing and prayer, discovery of spiritual gifts, serving one another, weeping with those who weep, and rejoicing with those who rejoice, are all part of the movement outward and preparation for ministry in the world.

Leadership and Discernment

Not all leadership is liberating leadership. Not everyone with natural leadership gifts is foundationally ready. Not everyone who thinks they are ready, are ready.

Identifying leaders and preparing them to serve involves spiritual discernment. Jonathan Edwards's *A Treatise Concerning Religious Affections* is fascinating for its delineation of spiritual effects from their semblances, providing us with "distinguishing signs of truly gracious and holy affections." He writes from his experience with revivals, which gave rise to various manifestations, not all of which were "spiritual." There are those whose seeming "religious affections" come without true knowledge of their need and without submission to God. "They allow God to be lovely in himself, no otherwise, than that he has forgiven them, and accepted them, and loves them above most in the world, and has engaged to improve all his infinite power and wisdom in preferring, dignifying and exalting them, and will do for them just as they would have him." These revival participants continue, after their "conversion," in the same self-absorbed ways, without recognition of their condition, but now with the sense that God has exalted them.[9] Frederick Douglass, a century after Jonathan Edwards, gives us a glimpse of what can hide beneath a false spirituality when he remarks on the effects of his slave master being converted at a Methodist camp meeting. Douglass expected that his master might emancipate his slaves (or at least treat them better), but things only got worse. "Prior to his conversion, he relied upon his own depravity to shield and sustain him in his savage barbarity; but after his conversion, he found religious sanction and support for his slaveholding cruelty."[10] The capacity of religion to mask evil remains pervasive.

We have to take seriously the religiosity that can cover a great deal of dysfunction in churches. Special care must be given to the spiritual sensibilities and visions of those put in charge of various ministries in the church. Not everyone who sees himself or herself as the right person for the job, is the right person. Often the people who deeply feel their inadequacy,

9. Edwards, *Religious Affections.*
10. Douglass, *Narrative,* 47.

and yet are open to God's call and empowering, are those that are ready to take up the task.

When it comes to electing a church council and being a council, "Robert's Rules of Order" do not rule. At St. Thomas, we picked up a suggestion from an article (whose title and author I do not recall) to form a prayer-nominating team. "Praying people" selected to this committee were given to understand that they were a prayer team; we provided guidance for prayerfully discerning leaders. Our position was that those who are being released outward, who understand the gospel of liberation, and who have a vision for the ever-widening circles of liberation, are in positions of leadership.

Discerning "gracious and holy affections" or, in other words, the liberating work of the Spirit, is critical for helping individuals along the journey and for the growth of the community in God's liberation. Where there is humility (a gracious affection), there is a desire for, and openness to, spiritual counsel. Where people acknowledge their need, and pray for each other and for whom God is their help, the word of truth is welcomed. Pastoral care involves speaking the truth in love, always acknowledging that the truth falls on the proclaimer as well. Spiritual direction with individuals and groups is critical for the deepening experience of God's liberation. Without shepherds other than the pastor, it is hard to imagine a congregation growing in numbers and in depth.

Ministry in Transition

If we are transitioning from being a social club church to a community of Jesus' followers moving outward in God's liberating work, we can expect the turbulence and conflict of change. It is critical for leaders to speak the truth in love, keep focused on the goal, and attend to the growth of those open to liberation (open to theirs and others). We are not going to fix things. Much is out of our control. Some fires that others start, we will be able to put out; some, however, will have to burn. It is important that the focus is on building up the body of Christ, as God frees us to be the concrete expression of Christ in the world, trusting God for guidance.

We proclaim the vision of God's liberating work, in season and out of season, and call the assembled believers to turn from that which keeps them from that work. We encourage them with the work of the Spirit who is with us in our turning, releasing us. We acknowledge God's work with gratitude and praise to God. We share with one another the joy of liberation. Those who resist are encouraged that this liberating life is for them as well, but their vision, formed by their addictions, cannot be affirmed. Those who are undergoing change must be nurtured and built up in God's liberating work. The middle-class-values captivity of the church must continue to be broken, and God's people liberated to serve as agents of freedom.

As this radical kind of change is taking place, some will leave. They will not see themselves in the church that is being raised up. However, it is not our responsibility to chase after them, to get them back to something they do not see for themselves (I learned this painfully, holding on to people I needed to let go). Choices are made. There is freedom to leave and freedom to stay. The liberated and liberating community is a creation of the Spirit, available for all. Our ministry is to all, both those who are committed to the outward movement of ministry and those who resist.

In all this, we, who are leaders, are daily reminded of our helplessness. The work we are engaged in is a work of God by the guidance and power of God, who is our help. We are radically dependent upon God for our own liberation, without which we are unable to recognize what true liberation looks like. Therefore, we come to God the only way we can: we come in our weakness. It is the way of the cross and, therefore, the way of prayer. By God's grace, light shines in our own lives to expose our addictions and idolatries. In the face of our false dependencies, we find we are helpless and dependent upon God's grace for the surrender of our wills to God. We share our journey with the people of God who are on the same journey. Together we wait upon God for the liberating work God does.

We stand with those who are on this journey and call others to it. We work to build up a community of liberation that becomes a model to others of God's purpose for those God gathers together. We encourage the witness of the liberated and liberating church that is emerging. We encourage liberating ministries. We seek out leaders for liberating worship. We seek to discern the gifts and ministries that the Spirit is stirring up for our ministry outward. All those in positions of leadership must see the church as open to all and ensure that those who come into the fellowship are received as family—that there is no series of hoops they must jump through in order to know they are welcome. We want those who decide to remain in the fellowship to do so in response to the call and word of God, proclaimed within a loving community where forgiveness is a prime ingredient.

Widening the Circle

But you will receive power when the Holy Spirit has come upon
you; and you will be my witnesses in Jerusalem, in all Judea and
Samaria, and to the ends of the earth. (Acts 1:8)

In many respects, the "ends of the earth" conceived in the first century
are now present everywhere through global communications, as well as
through migrations that have created great diversity (especially in urban
centers). It is becoming increasingly apparent that distance from the other
is a matter of the openness of our hearts. The widening of the circle for the
outward movement of God's people, whether urban, rural or suburban, has
to do with our ability to recognize the needs of others by hearing their cries.
Again, the problem is predominantly spiritual.

Leadership that is working with those who are undergoing spiritual
transformation and gaining ears to hear must be intentional about helping
others to hear the cries. We must pay attention to the cries in forums and
Bible studies and prayer gatherings and sermons and community organizations. There must be a mobilization directed to the needs of others; this
starts with listening. It is striking to note the extent to which whites living distant from the reality of black life can have much to say about what
they think black people *ought* to be doing. People with little knowledge
of Islam can nevertheless proclaim all kinds of judgments concerning this
religion. It is when we truly realize that "it's me, it's me standing in the need
of prayer; not my brother, not my sister but it's me," that we begin to have
ears that actually hear what others are expressing. We come as needy people
to other needy people. We *need* the cries of those who are experiencing oppression, in order to begin to understand and to change, and to know how
to respond from wherever we are located.

The collection Paul took up among largely Gentile churches for Christians in Jerusalem implies that he shared with them the poverty of the Jerusalem church. They then had the opportunity to respond. Pastors and
leaders today have a similar obligation. The need is not always economic,
but often heavy burdens of one form or another; the call is to be salt, light,
and yeast, working for change in our society and world. Congregations
begin by listening. So, for example, a congregation could offer a series dedicated to understanding the mass incarceration of people of color in America.[11] The goal would be directed toward response: in what ways can our

11. Many denominations provide social statements for their congregations. The

congregation be an agent of change? We expect that God has something to say to us through the cries. There is a word of the Lord to God's people for doing justice in specific, concrete ways. Those being liberated and having "ears to hear" will respond.

Pastors can help their members gain greater hearing ability, both to human cries and God's Spirit, by helping them recognize their attitudes toward the other. The sermon is the primary means for this. Both text and life provide ample opportunities. We can have the gathered people reflect on their attitudes toward other ethnicities, religions, genders, and sexual orientations. Further, we can encourage them to reflect on their attitudes toward the poor, the incarcerated, the addicted, the victim, the perpetrator, the rioter, the protester, and so on. When do they experience empathy, mercy, and a desire to respond to need? When do they feel moved to judgment and condemnation, disgust and anger? What brings forth understanding and solidarity? What is God's response to these same groups? What kind of welcome do we encounter in Jesus, who said to the very religious people of his day, "I assure you that tax collectors [traitors] and prostitutes are entering God's kingdom ahead of you"?[12] God's people have attitudes from which they must repent, as well as repenting from the source of those attitudes in the idolatry of self. The more we realize that there is no difference between us and others in this common condition, the more we can join others in receiving God's forgiveness and liberation.

In previous chapters, I have kept as a common example the experience of racism and white privilege. Racism has been called "America's original sin." It formed the basis for the kind of slavery practiced in the Americas. It elaborated a philosophy and theology of white superiority as a basis for white supremacy. Its legacy continued after slavery's abolishment, through persistent Jim Crow laws made possible through decisions made by the Supreme Court, undermining civil rights amendments enacted following the civil war.[13] More recently, its continued legacy is manifest in the weakening of civil rights legislation—in particular, the Voting Rights Act. That same racism has been behind legislation that resulted in criminal justice actions bringing about the mass incarceration of people of color and the poor. It

Evangelical Lutheran Church in America offers an excellent statement on the criminal justice system. Using this statement and reading it together with Michelle Alexander's *The New Jim Crow*, a forum for understanding can be created.

12. Matt 21:31.

13. For an examination of Supreme Court decisions following the Civil War, see Goldstone, *Inherently Unequal*.

is seen in the way policing is done in communities of color and the way children of color are treated. The legacy of slavery and racism remains a virulent force in our society, causing great harm and injustice. It is clear that racism remains an addiction and disease and sin for white people, including white Christians. Consequently, it is not ignored by the word of God.

God addresses our idolatry of race and ethnicity, calling us to repent. For that word to be heard, proclaimers must make it plain, in concrete and specific terms, for hearers of the word. The word must be directed clearly to our bondage, an addiction insidious in its denial. Proclaimers must make it personal, with illustrations from both our own experience and that of others. Making it plain, we trust the Spirit to convince. We call for the repentance that bears the fruit of confession: making amends and taking action that effects change in our congregations and our society. In this addiction, as well as others, the word along with the Spirit is the agent of change. Consequently, proclaimers must continually turn away from believing in the power of brokenness—ours and others—to believing in the power of the word and the power of God. Belief that our idolatrous condition is impenetrable and unchangeable is a persistent temptation. Only as hearers of the word do proclaimers also grow in faith.

We are all on a journey with a diversity of gifts and callings, leadership among them. We all stand before the same word, dependent on the same Spirit for help and in need of the prayers of God's people. That same word continues to call each of us to repentance and faith, a daily turning from idols to serve God. That turning is always a gift; it comes by the grace of God.

9

Grace

OUR BEING RELEASED OUTWARD is by the grace of God. It is a gift. All that we are and all that we have is a gift. All of creation is graced.

In her book *Christ in Evolution*, Ilia Delio refers to Joseph Sittler as initiating the modern discussion of a cosmic Christology at the General Assembly of the World Council of Churches in New Delhi in 1961.[1] He raised up the notion of the cosmic Christ both there and in his subsequent book, *Essays on Nature and Grace*, where he reflects on the cosmic Christ of Colossians and Ephesians. He summarized the theology of grace in the Eastern tradition (divinization, recapitulation—which included the entire created order and the maturation of the human being) and the Western tradition including the Reformation (grace as God's response to sin and guilt). Then he addressed the broader reality of grace, as present in Scripture and tradition, which is necessary in the present moment. While his underlying concern is for the way nature is left out of notions of grace (and the implications for ecology), his discussion opens up the wideness of grace for the full range of human experience.

Beyond "grace as primarily an overcoming of alienation from God by God's action of forgiveness," he asks about grace as a "sheer phenomenon." As such, grace is the "sheer givenness-character of life, the world and the self—the plain presentedness of all that is." He notes that "the term 'gratuity of grace' includes both the knowledge of the gift and the astonishment that all that is is 'gifted.'"[2] Sittler believes that grace must be understood in

1. Delio, *Christ in Evolution*, chapter 2, section 1, subsection 3.
2. Sittler, *Essays on Nature and Grace*, 88.

terms of the fullness of the Trinity—as the grace of creator, redeemer, and sanctifier. As such, grace is the expression of God's love.

God's grace is experienced in the gift of life itself, in the revelation of God in the flesh, joined to our humanity, in God's entering into our suffering and brokenness and as present in our coming to be. If we set aside for a moment the reality of sin and consider humanity as it comes to be, grows, and matures into itself as made in the image of God, we find we are attending to God incarnate, present and embodied in God's creation. We see God's grace in Christ, the Logos, made flesh, dwelling in God's creation, inherent in our coming to be our true selves. When we include our experience of sin, we discover the significance of the cross, not only in our dying to earlier forms of what we are coming to be, but dying to our false selves that have emanated from our attempts—in our radical freedom—to structure our lives without God.

If we think of grace in this way, then we may also speak, as Karl Rahner does, of a graced transcendentality. Our transcendental openness to God, from whom we have come, is also an openness to God, given to us in the expression of God in Christ (in the flesh) and, therefore, in our humanity. We experience that gracious giving as we welcome, in trusting faith, God graciously given to us. That welcome is also a welcome of our true humanity, as created for God, to receive God. We understand this welcome as the experience of the Spirit of God, who enables us to say "yes" to the gift of God, given by God.

This incarnating, reconciling work of God in Christ, expressed in this way, means that the gift of God's presence in the gift of creation, our coming to be and growth in God, our welcome and forgiveness, the gift of the Spirit, our vocation and works of love are one reality which is all gift. The gift of forgiveness is implied in our liberation, which is a gift. Our becoming instruments of God's holistic liberating work is a gift. Our being released outward is a gift.

I recall a Lutheran seminary professor excluding the word "must" from the language of grace as if the *necessity* to decide or to act goes against God's freely given salvation. And yet there is a necessity attached to our deciding to be our true selves—or, in other words, in our letting ourselves be who God is creating us to be. Our deciding, our "letting go," is a life and death matter. If we desire to live and to be who God created us to be, it is necessary to be liberated from that which keeps us from our true selves in God. "Truly I tell you, unless you change and become like children, you will never enter the kingdom of heaven."[3] "Unless you repent, you will all perish as they did."[4] It is necessary to turn to God and change. We *must* repent. When we do, we realize repentance is a gift. It is by God's grace that we come to repentance. We realize it was not our doing, but the gift of God. Yet, we experienced the "must," the necessity of deciding, of taking a step, of letting go of ourselves to God's gift and work in us.

I have seen this many times with recovering drug addicts. They would say that until they were *willing* to let go of the drug, there was no change—but, that was the dilemma. They had to let go of that which held their will against their will. That is why, in the testimony of many, there was something that brought them to a place of great pain and helplessness. "I spent my money on drugs, rather than food for my child." "I stole from my daughter." "I held up a store for drug money." (This addict immediately put himself into treatment when he realized how far he had fallen.) "I almost died." "I am tired of living on the street." At the point of helplessness, when they despaired of their own actions, God's gift of liberation was waiting for them. By God's grace, they were freed to turn their lives over to God as they knew God.

The reality of God's grace, God's lavish giving, opens the door to life. The grace-filled community provides a welcome and a confidence in God's giving for weary, burdened people who have lost hope. Among *believers* who rejoice in God's liberating power freely given, words of faith and confident hope are shared: "God can do for you what you have been unable to do for yourself." There are those in the community who will pray for those who have lost faith and will continue to pray, believing for them, until they themselves are able to believe again.

It is by God's grace that such a community is raised up. It is by God's grace that the gift of God's love is poured into hearts by the Holy Spirit. It is because of God's liberation, freely given, from addictions and idols, that we are released to see the needs of others and are sent out. It is by God's grace that we come to care about the good of all. It is by God's grace that we recognize our need in such a way that we are no longer inclined to judge others. We are all in need of God's good gifts.

It is by God's grace that we listen to others until we begin to understand. It is by God's grace that, understanding, we respond as the Spirit

3. Matt 18:3.
4. Luke 13:3.

leads. We hear the cries and take action. For the one who needs healing, we pray for healing. For the one who confesses and repents from sin, we speak God's word of forgiveness. For the one who is being oppressed, we "undo the thongs of the yoke, to let the oppressed go free, and to break every yoke," including systemic and institutional yokes.[5] For those who are oppressing, we speak the truth of God's judgment, "Come now, you rich people, weep and wail for the miseries that are coming to you." And we call out the injustice: "The wages of the laborers who mowed your fields, which you kept back by fraud, cry out, and the cries of the harvesters have reached the ears of the Lord of hosts."[6] We are freed to do justice, love mercy, and walk faithfully—and all this is by grace.

God's grace cannot be relegated simply to forgiveness for personal sin, as wonderful as that is. Grace takes in the whole of God's giving. The community of faith, which experiences the multi-faceted reality of God's grace, becomes involved in a variety of ministries, as there are a variety of needs. When there is need for forgiveness, the community knows God's mercy. When there is need for healing, the community knows God's power. When there is need for deliverance from addiction, repentance from idols, comfort for those who mourn, healing for inner hurts, justice for those oppressed, witness against oppressive ways, the community knows there is "grace to help in time of need."[7]

God's grace is present for ever-widening circles of liberation. God gives us what we need to be light in the world, to be witnesses and change agents on behalf of Christ and in Christ. There is grace for every work of liberation. There is grace for working out our own liberation, "for it is God who is at work in [us], enabling [us] both to will and to work for his good pleasure."[8] There is grace for organizing and joining with others in acts of agitation and confrontation, for the sake of justice. There is grace to work for change in entrenched, unjust systems, to endure many losses on the path to change and to be faithful in our witness. There is grace for compassion for the broken-hearted, the excluded, the victims, the imprisoned, and the abused. There are gifts of grace for entering into the lives of others, for the sake of serving them. There is grace for giving ourselves for the

5. Isa 58:6.
6. Jas 5:1, 4.
7. Heb 4:16.
8. Phil 2:12–13.

common good as yeast that is present and works to affect the whole. There is grace to lose our lives for Christ and the gospel.

God, enlighten the eyes of our hearts, that we may know your liberating work "according to the riches of [your] grace that [you] lavished on us."[9]

9. Eph 1:7–8.

Bibliography

Alexander, Michelle. *The New Jim Crow: Mass Incarceration in the Age of Colorblindness.* New York: New Press, 2012.

Baker, Bruce D. "America's Most Financially Disadvantaged School Districts and How They Got That Way; How State and Local Governance Causes School Funding Disparities." https://cdn.americanprogress.org/wp-content/uploads/2014/07/Baker SchoolDistricts.pdf.

Barth, Karl. *The Word of God and the Word of Man.* Translated by Douglas Horton. Gloucester, MA: Peter Smith, 1978.

Bonhoeffer, Dietrich. *The Collected Sermons of Dietrich Bonhoeffer.* Edited by Isabel Best. Minneapolis: Fortress, 2012.

———. *Dietrich Bonhoeffer Works, Volume 8: Letters and Papers from Prison.* Edited by Christian Gremmels, Eberhard Bethge, and John W. de Grutchy. Translated by Isabel Best, Lisa E. Dahill, Reinhard Krauss, and Nancy Lukens. Minneapolis: Fortress, 2010.

———. *Spiritual Care.* Translated by Jay C. Rochelle. Philadelphia: Fortress, 1985.

———. *A Testament To Freedom: The Essential Writings of Dietrich Bonhoeffer.* Edited by Geffrey B. Kelly, and F. Burton Nelson. New York: HarperCollins, 1990.

Delio, Ilia. *Christ in Evolution.* Maryknoll, NY: Orbis, 2008. Kindle edition.

Douglass, Frederick. *The Life and Times of Frederick Douglass.* New York: Firework, 2015.

———. *Narrative Of The Life Of Frederick Douglass An American Slave.* Boston: Anti-Slavery Office, 1845.

Edwards, Jonathan. *Religious Affections, Works of Jonathan Edwards Online.* Vol. 2. Yale University: Jonathan Edwards Center, 2008. http://edwards.yale.edu.

Evangelical Lutheran Worship; Pastoral Care. Minneapolis: Augsburg Fortress, 2008.

Foster, Richard J. *Streams of Living Water: Celebrating the Great Traditions of Christian Faith.* New York: HarperCollins, 1998.

Goldstone, Lawrence. *Inherently Unequal: The Betrayal of Equal Rights by the Supreme Court, 1865–1903.* New York: Walker & Company, 2011.

Hays, Richard B. *The Faith of Jesus Christ: The Narrative Substructure of Galatians 3:1–4:11.* Second Edition. Grand Rapids, MI: William B. Eerdmans, 2002.

Joyce, Ann Mercer. "Feminism and Womanist Practical Theology." In *Opening the Field of Practical Theology; An Introduction,* edited by Kathleen A. Cahalan and Gordon S. Mikoski, 97–114. Lanham, MD: Rowman & Littlefield, 2014.

Kärkkäinen, Veli-Matti. *One with God: Salvation as Deification and Justification.* Collegeville, MN: Liturgical, 2004.

Bibliography

Kelly, Joseph T. *Saint Augustine of Hippo: Selections from Confessions and Other Essential Writings, Annotated & Explained Edition*. Nashville: Skylight Paths, 2010.

Kilcrease, Jack D., and Erwin W. Lutzer, eds. *Martin Luther In His Own Words; Essential Writings of the Reformation*. Grand Rapids, MI: Baker, 2017.

Kozol, Jonathan. *Savage Inequalities: Children in America's Schools*. New York: Crown, 1991.

Luther, Martin. *Preface to the Letter of St. Paul to the Romans*. Translated by Andrew Thornton. http://www.ccel.org/l/luther/romans/pref_romans.html.

Mannermaa, Tuomo. *Christ Present in Faith: Martin Luther's View of Justification*. Edited by Kirsi Stjerna. Minneapolis: Fortress, 2005.

May, Gerald G. *Addiction & Grace*. New York: HarperCollins, 1988.

Miller-McLemore, Bonnie J., ed. *The Wiley-Blackwell Companion to Practical Theology*. Chichester, UK: Blackwell, 2012.

Niebuhr, Reinhold. *Moral Man and Immoral Society: A Study in Ethics and Politics*. Louisville: Westminster John Knox, 2013.

Pero, Albert. "Worship and Theology in the Black Context." In *Theology and the Black Experience*, edited by Albert Pero and Ambrose Moyo, 227–48. Minneapolis: Augsburg, 1988.

Rahner, Karl. *The Dynamic Element in the Church*. New York: Herder and Herder, 1964.

———. *Foundations of Christian Faith; An Introduction to the Idea of Christianity*. Translated by William V. Dych. New York: Seabury, 1978.

———. *Theological Investigations*. Vol. 9. Translated by Graham Harrison. London: Darton, Longman & Todd, 1972.

Rohr, Richard. *Eager to Love: The Alternative Way of Francis of Assisi*. Cincinnati: Franciscan Media, 2014.

———. *Immortal Diamond: The Search for Our True Self*. San Francisco: Jossey-Bass, 2013.

Root, Andrew. *Christopraxis: A Practical Theology of the Cross*. Minneapolis: Fortress, 2014.

Sanna, Ellyn. *All Shall Be Well; A Modern Language Version of the Revelation of Julian of Norwich*. New York: Harding, 2011. Kindle edition.

Sider, Ronald J. *The Early Church on Killing: A Comprehensive Sourcebook on War, Abortion, and Capital Punishment*. Grand Rapids, MI: BakerAcademic, 2012.

Sittler, Joseph. *Essays on Nature and Grace*. Philadelphia: Fortress, 1972.

Smith, Kenneth L., and Ira G. Zepp Jr. *Search for the Beloved Community; The Thinking of Martin Luther King Jr*. Valley Forge, PA: Judson, 1998.

Tillich, Paul. *Dynamics of Faith*. New York: Harper & Row, 1957.

Tolstoy, Leo. *Resurrection*. Translated by Louise Maude. Ware, UK: Wordsworth, 2014.

Williams, Reggie L. *Bonhoeffer's Black Jesus; Harlem Renaissance Theology and an Ethic of Resistance*. Waco, TX: Baylor University Press, 2014. Kindle edition.

Wright, N.T. *Justification: God's Plan & Paul's Vision*. Downers Grove, IL: IVP Academic, 2009.

Zumbach, Lauren, and Susan DeMar Lafferty. "New School Funding Bill Won't Change Much." *Chicago Tribune Daily Southtown Newspaper*, April 3, 2015.

www.ingramcontent.com/pod-product-compliance
Lightning Source LLC
Chambersburg PA
CBHW070457090426
42735CB00012B/2588